The 7 Gears Between Cause & Effect

This one's for You!

Thomas K. Tolman

THE 7 GEARS
BETWEEN
CAUSE & EFFECT

CAUSE

EFFECT

GAINING MASTERY OVER YOUR *OUTCOMES*,
RESULTS, AND *CONDITIONS!*

THOMAS TOLMAN

The 7 Gears

Between Cause & Effect

Gaining Mastery Over Your Outcomes,
Results, and Conditions!

Thomas K. Tolman

Illustrated by Donald Tolman

Author: Thomas Kent Tolman

Title: **The 7 Gears Between Cause & Effect**

Subtitle: *Gaining Mastery Over Your Outcomes, Results & Conditions!*

Edition: First Edition

U.S. place of publication: Raleigh, NC

Published by: Lulu Press, Inc.

Value B&W Edition

Copyright © 2015 Thomas Kent Tolman

Graphic artwork, Cog the character, the 7 Gear symbol, Perform-O-Stat, The Collaboration Continuum, and the term Cogno-Kinetics are registered trademarks exclusive to the 7Gears book, The 7 Gears Program, and are owned by T.K.Tolman, LLC.

The 7 Gears Program

Arvada, Colorado 80005

www.the7Gears.com

Dedicated to Carwin Delos Tolman, my dad,

who sold me on the value of study!

ACKNOWLEDGEMENTS

To my son, Donald Tolman, Illustrator extraordinaire, Format and Print Editor, for his endless patience and creativity in working with me through untold iterations. To my daughter, Jennifer Kate Tolman, Marketing Manager and Coach, for her wisdom and defined direction on critical details, valuable insight and loving sustained support throughout. To my son Kevin and his wife, Rania, who contributed expert insight as well as valuable perspective and feedback, throughout. To the countless individuals who voted on the best cover design, again and again, I am sincerely thankful to you. Special thanks to Janeyl, Berenise, Angie and Kattian Tellez, who have provided great ongoing support and insight. To Mr. Marty Cooper, "Father of the Cellphone"—thank you for the great interview in LaJolla, CA. Special thanks to Shelley Buchwald, Chief Editor and advisor, for her perseverance, patience and exceptional talent. I am very grateful for the loving support and ongoing encouragement from my wife and soul mate, Jeanette, who has always believed in me and inspired me to get started and follow through on this two-year project.

TABLE OF CONTENTS

PART ONE
CAUSE

The Area of Any Possibility, Any Opportunity
First and Secondary Causes

PART TWO
THE 7 GEARS

The 1st Gear: Your Knowledge-Transfer Medium
Sensory Acuity
The Six Higher Faculties of the Human Mind
Two Levels of Awareness
Attention! May I Have Your Attention?
The Light of Attention
Conscious Mind
Subconscious Mind
Levels of Consciousness
Level and Direction of Awareness

What is an Operating System-Blueprint?
What Operating Version Are You?
Stages of Life
Change the Menu
Reprogramming Your Mind (System) for Upgraded Results
Destiny-Shaping Tools
Values–Purpose–Goals–Identity

PART THREE
EFFECT

EPILOGUE

REFERENCES

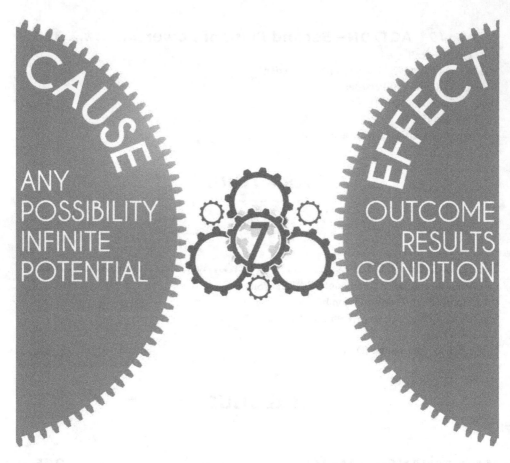

Align and connect unlimited opportunities and potential

to exciting outcomes and results

"We all know that the law of cause and effect is inviolable, yet how many of us ever pause to consider its workings?"

– Claude M. Bristol[1]

PREFACE

Are you ready to get your life into a higher gear? Then know right here, right now that **you** are your best investment.

When working toward your goals, have you ever felt you were barely treading water, just dog paddling your way along, with very little progress? Advancing toward our goals can often feel like jumping into an Olympic-sized swimming pool with weights on and trying to swim to the other end and back. What if you suddenly were equipped with the right tools, such as flippers, snorkel, wetsuit, head-cap and a motorized propelling device? Wouldn't all of that equipment make the challenge much easier? What started out to be a daunting task could actually become fun. Having the right tools for the task at hand can make the difference between success and failure.

I believe we are all here to find ways to express our unique skills and talents, and to promote the overall good of the world around us. Though we may be born with gifts and abilities, they need to be discovered and nurtured in order to flourish. No matter where we are in life, whether it's on the streets living from hand to mouth, or in a 10,000-square-foot house with a $500,000/year income, all of us want to make progress and continue to advance in improving our condition, our standard of living. I don't believe that this is a matter of greed, but rather something our

11

Creator has intentionally placed deep within our being. There is something inherent in our souls that yearns to climb the highest mountain. We want to get the promotion, win the contest, the race, the lotto, or the argument. In this century, this inborn trait has evolved into an insatiable curiosity to explore the deepest reaches of space, invent more efficient cars, and land on other planets and worlds. Sometimes our goals are more personal: we just want to find a way to get our children through college or save for the next vacation. At a foundational level, we simply want to improve, advance, grow, and accomplish!

One of the greatest movies of all time, *The Wizard of Oz*, depicts each character overcoming a personal problem and obtaining his or her wants and desires. I think one of the primary reasons it has an everlasting appeal is that we can all relate at some level to the struggles and challenges along the way on our own yellow brick road. Hope springs eternal, and we resonate with hope meeting success. It is my hope that in this book you will find at least one valuable viewpoint or concept that resonates with you and provides a missing puzzle piece in this amazing quest for life advancement and growth that we are all on.

The process of building something requires equipment, tools, and an effective procedure. Successfully accomplishing goals is no different, since tools and equipment are not limited to the physical realm; they can also be mental in nature. We all need the right knowledge, training and skills to effectively use tools to get the job done correctly. This book delves into 7 big ones. Tools, that is. Each of the 7 gears you'll read about are actually more than tools; they are essential factors I refer to as GEARS. These interactive gears operate *in between* causes and their resulting effects or outcomes. These gears represent seven human endowments given to us as tools to use in making our way through this world. The purpose of this book is to raise your awareness and understanding of the seven gear elements embedded in the great law of Cause and Effect. I want to empower you with the tools, ideas, insights and hidden rules that, if understood and applied in the right way *and* in the right order, can create real and lasting change.

Computers function and perform at a certain level according to their operating system. You have a much more advanced and marvelous operating system than any computer on the planet, with your own physical, mental, and emotional knowledge-processing subsystems. Most operating systems require occasional upgrades to improve their performance. This book focuses on the 7 key elements that are required for your "system upgrade" so that you may operate at peak potential and performance. *The 7 Gears Between Cause and Effect* is about equipping you with the knowledge, skill, ability and wisdom to get to wherever you want to go. Are you ready for this adventure?

INTRODUCTION

My dad once said, "Son, study! Study people, and study what works." He was describing today's buzz word: modeling. Dad's advice to me was, "If you want to move ahead farther, faster, then start by learning and applying the value of studying. If you want more successful outcomes, then study success!" And so I set off on a lifelong journey of attending every seminar I could and reading hundreds of self-improvement books.

I started my personal improvement library when I was 17 with a book I ordered through the mail (not online; this was the era of 45 RPM records!) titled *Your Thoughts Can Change Your Life*, by Donald Curtis. I read and re-read that book, but I didn't resonate with it or understand the depth of his viewpoints. However, I was intrigued by the title. If success really did leave clues, then I wanted in on the hunt. I studied other books, including the king of success books, Napoleon Hill's 1937 classic, *Think and Grow Rich*. The more I read and studied, the more I knew there had to be something affecting one's level of success other than simply having a positive attitude, setting goals, maintaining focus, or, as Rocky Balboa said to Apollo Creed, simply going for it! However, much of the material I read was incomplete or ineffective because key information was lacking or because I failed to apply the tools or techniques called for. Not because I didn't believe it was good, but because my motivation level was weak, and then a life distraction pulled my attention away.

The All Important

Over the years I have sifted through the best ideas, tools, and principles and have assembled what I believe to be the key factors in controlling outcomes and influencing life experiences for the better. While there has been much talk about the Law of Attraction, I am more intrigued by the Law of Cause and Effect. I have been curious and perplexed as to why some people move ahead while others don't. What I have discovered are 7 factors—I call them Gears—that operate **between** Cause and Effect. These gears are the key causes that add up and culminate in our outcomes, conditions, results, and, ultimately, our destiny.

Many of us have been told by well-meaning parents, teachers, and instructors that we have unlimited potential. They have said that knowledge is power, that we only use 10% of our brain, that we should seize the day. We hear that fortune favors the bold and that we must take responsibility. This is all true and all useful. But I've found that distilling these great truths down to their core fundamentals and then properly sequencing them exponentially boosts the real power they deliver in our lives.

"Yeah, I've heard of Cause and Effect. So what?"

Expanding Your Toolkit for Achievement

Have you ever seen the popular bumper sticker that says, "S— happens"? Well, yes "stuff" does happen, but has anyone asked *why?* There is a reason for everything. A person's financial worth, physical health, relationships, and career are all exactly what they are for one or more reasons. We live in a universe of cause and effect, but we pay too much attention to effects and not enough to causes. Like events in the physical universe, failure and success also have causes and effects. If we can get at the heart of reasons, the "why" of an outcome, then we can use that knowledge to influence and change results we're not happy with.

Authors Viktor Frankl and Steven R. Covey brought to light the universal human endowment that there is a *space of choice* between what happens to you and what you do about it. YOU decide your response to every event or experience.[2] Just knowing this is powerful. My discovery was that there is also a *space* between Cause and Effect. There are 7 gears, or factors, between Cause and Effect, and you have the ability to access, control, and decide how you will use them to your

16

benefit. Pause for a minute and ponder the significance of this! Right now you should be on the edge of your seat!

In the game of Blackjack, there are certain strategies you can use to increase the odds of a winning hand. Knowing when to hit, stand, double down or split can help you, depending on your hand and what the dealer's up card is. We've all been dealt a certain hand of cards from birth, such as where we live, our standard of living, our family, home life, and hereditary factors, to name a few. The exciting thing about the game of life is that you can change some of the cards in your hand. There are strategies and approaches you can take to improve your odds of having a "winning hand" in life.

Change the Causes, Change the Effects

Any success, however you define it, demands focused, sustained exertion. You have to decide to go after it and maintain sufficient drive to persist to completion.

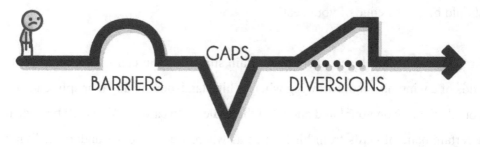

BARRIERS   GAPS   DIVERSIONS

There are barriers, gaps, and what I call diversions, between where you are and where you want to be. Just having the drive and energy is not enough; you must follow certain principles. Yes, success leaves clues, but it also has rules. Just as the construction of any material thing requires following certain universal laws, there must be adherence to the laws of success. What we're talking about here is utilizing the great Law of Cause and Effect to our advantage. And that's where the 7 Gears come in! The purpose of this book is to give you the best and most useful concepts, tools, and insights into certain Causes, so that you can attain one or more of the following Effects with greater probability:

- Success
- Wealth
- Health
- Happiness
- Sense of well being
- Purpose—with clarity and conviction
- Confidence and wisdom to influence more favorable results
- Making real progress; making the difference you seek
- Life experience rewards
- Peace of mind
- Emotional and financial freedom
- Positive influence
- Thought clarity
- More goals realized, and sooner
- Willpower that works
- Financial and emotional security

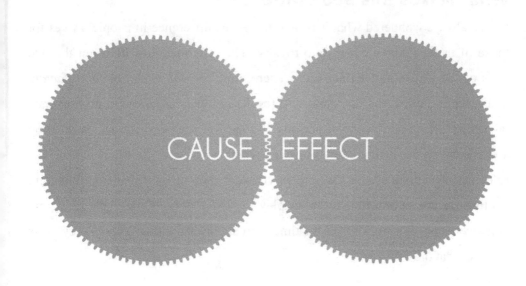

CAUSE EFFECT

By Accident or Intention?

What is the Difference that Makes the Difference in the Quality of our Life Experiences?

As far back as I can remember, I recall hearing phrases like "mind over matter," but it took years for me to understand the significance of that simple phrase. I eventually realized the power and potential of the concept that *thoughts are causes* in all human endeavors. James Allen says, "Cause and effect is absolute and undeviating in the hidden realm of thought as in the world of visible and material things. Mind is the master weaver, both of the interior garment of character and the outer garment of circumstance."[3] In other words, **every outcome, result, or condition in your life has a reason behind it.** Certain eternal, omnipresent laws govern the universe we live in. Everything happens for a reason. What I finally realized was that these happenings can serve us!

What Makes this Book Different?

I have always wondered what it is that makes the difference in people's lives for those of us who weren't born into royalty. The difference lies **between** the two ends of the **Cause and Effect Law.** There are *changeable, controllable factors* that steer and direct the outcomes and results in our lives. As with all universal laws, this law is no respecter of persons. It doesn't matter who you are, where you are, when you get it figured out, or even whether you ever do figure it out. The rules and functions of this law are in constant motion by default or intention, waiting for you at any time to either play the game or have the game play you. However, since it's working all the time, you are always either at the mercy of its effects, or at the controls.

Why Gears?

One of the reasons I've used the metaphoric term "gears" instead of "building blocks" or "steps" is because these 7 interactive factors are more than just steps. Steps are more like mini platforms or passive positions. A step can be an action, but it doesn't contain the moving interactive elements of a gear. Gears transfer *internal* energy and power from one source to a forward-moving function, like a finely tuned watch or a car transmission. As you will see, 5 ½ of the 7 gears run internally within all of us. You will discover that seeing the world from this perspective will give you an empowering advantage that will make the difference in getting you to your goal-outcomes faster and more completely.

Missing Pieces = Incomplete Picture

We are all works in progress, and some of us need more work on our progress. This book does not have *all* the answers, but the exclusive order and sequence should, if sincerely applied, give you a distinct advantage In experiencing the outcomes and conditions you seek. As with a combination lock or a recipe, you must have not only the right ingredients, but also the right order of steps.

This book is not so much a how-to book, but rather a combination why-to, where-to, and when-to book. Like any recipe or formula, it demonstrates the importance of **what success factor goes where, and when, and why**. In keeping to the Cause and Effect theme, **reasons come before the answers**, and it's the micro-mini causes that stack up to drive and deliver the outcomes and conditions we experience. The purpose of this book is to enlighten, empower, and align your thought-causes toward more rewarding effects and outcomes. Our thought and habit patterns determine what we are and what we will be in the future because they direct and steer our actions, and that's what shapes our destiny.

The Mission of *The 7 Gears* is Threefold:

1) To help you become the *best version of yourself;*
2) To give you *a better working achievement system* that lets you tap into the unlimited opportunities waiting for you and convert them to a new exciting level of life experiences;
3) To reveal *the inner working factors* between Cause and Effect so you can systematically activate and align your true capacity and fullest potential to life- changing results and outcomes.

The 7 gears you are about to learn are not complex, but they are essential to getting life-changing results. If internalized and applied, they can give you the "house advantage" to influencing achievements, results, and effects in your favor! If "luck" is where preparation meets opportunity, then let's get in gear and go after those opportunities!

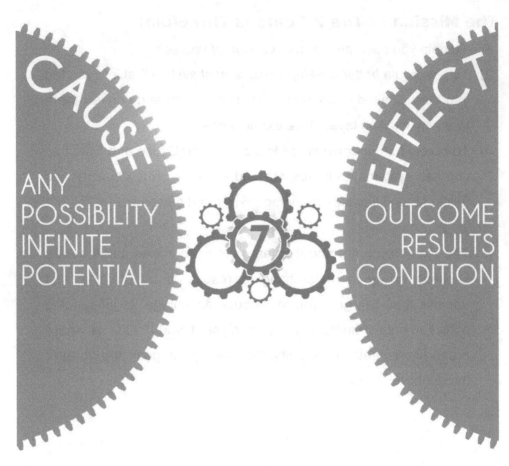

The 7 Gears is about Gears as Dynamic-Interactive Factors

This Book is Predicated on a Few Central Factors:

– Many people just aren't aware of any links, or connecting aspects between cause and effect, nor do they understand the importance of its interacting elements.

- Our life objective paths don't always travel a straight line from point A to point B because each of us is continuously confronted with barriers, gaps and diversions.

- We live in a universe of order that is governed by invisible, powerful laws that line up in harmony like a smoothly running transmission.

- Everything under the sun is subject to a lifecycle—an ongoing transition—that is always in a fluid state of either creation or decay.

- Yes, "stuff" happens to us all, but change begins first within, then progresses outward, and it is always our decision.

- When you learn and apply the 7 Gears that control and change outcomes and effects, you will increase the odds in your favor toward reaching more of your full potential, and you will increase your access to bigger and better opportunities.

- These 7 Gears will give you the traction and horsepower you need to bust through barriers, leap over gaps, and avoid detours and delays to get you to your destination faster and on target.

- All human beings contain genius capacity at some level, in some way—and that includes you!

Everything is in Motion

As we move through our life stages, we are all moving vehicles, so to speak. So what kind of vehicle are you? What's your horsepower, mileage per gallon, and fuel octane? Do you have tires with good tread and a 4-wheel drive to handle slippery spots? Do you have a map in your glove box or a GPS system? Do your gauges work so you can monitor your vehicle's vital signs? Do you have Xenon headlights to see in the dark and stay on your path? Reduced to a simple formula: At the present moment, we are **the sum** (full effect) **of our positive and negative working gears**. It's always a matter of what power factor, positive or negative, outnumbers or outweighs the other side.

We operate on the sum of our positive and negative running gears

Nothing in life stays the same. **Everything is in motion,** things visible and those at a subatomic level, most of which are out of range of our five senses. We are either moving forward or backsliding. There is no in-between. *The 7 Gears* brings together the right combination of gears, connecting one to the other. It's the transmission that transfers power to your wheels, which then moves you forward.

Why 7 Gears between Cause and Effect?

All references to the gears go beyond the traditional range of physics and the interactions of matter, energy, and motion. The drive and function of each gear is infused with the additional element of mental, emotional, spiritual energy such as the light of awareness, knowledge, skill, and ability. You may notice an unusual looking positioning of the gears in the above illustration. That's because 5½ of the gears run in the invisible internal level, and 1½ run in the physical external level of existence. The positioning of these gears is extremely important and will be explained in more depth in subsequent chapters.

There is a common manifesting mantra known as *be–do–have*. From a higher vantage point, gears 1 through 6 are the **"BE"** gears, **Gear 7** is the **"DO"** gear, and **"HAVE"** is the outcomes and effects gear. Each gear or principle functions in many ways like a real gear: 1. It **transfers power** energy from one point to another. 2. It **requires alignment** and lubrication to work most efficiently. 3. It requires **finely engineered** cogs that fit the contact mesh points. 4. Its purpose is to **transfer power from an originating source to an end goal** function, similar to a car transmission that transfers engine torque power to the axle and wheels.

Mental-Emotional Mechanics

You will be learning about the order and placement of these 7 factors and elements. This procession of primary and supplemental causes moves as a Cybernetic-Mind Mechanic type of operation. Cybernetics is the study of communication and control processes in biological, mechanical, and electronic systems. Cybernetics comes from the Greek derivation "to navigate or govern, to steer or control." And that's exactly what we're interested in here: learning and determining just how much control we as humans actually have between causes and effects! But there's more to it than just cybernetics. We're going to focus on 2 subsets of cybernetics: **cognitive** and **kinetic** processes.

Cogno-Kinetics

Cogno-Kinetics is a term I've coined that characterizes how the 7 Gears function. The word cognition comes from the Latin verb "cognosco," meaning "I know, perceive, or recognize." **Cognition** is the study of the mind and its processes, whether it's through psychology, philosophy, or neuroscience. Thought processes such as attention, memory, judgment, evaluating, reasoning, computation, problem solving, and decision making are all parts of cognition. You could call it information processing.

Kinetics is the energy of motion, or supplying a motive force. Any object that is in motion has kinetic energy. That energy can be vibratory or rotational like a flywheel. Kinetic energy can be transferred from one object to another, such as when a pool cue ball strikes another ball. **Cogno-Kinetics** is the intelligent systematic alignment of each gear as it transfers energy and momentum into the next gear, ultimately surfacing and transitioning from the mental realm into the physical realm as visible, tangible action. The quality and results of each action are then manifested as outcomes, results or conditions; in other words, effects. Hence **Cogno-Kinetics** is the concept behind the 7 Gears process.

The Combination that Opens the Door

So how do we gain access to the success we seek? Having the right combination is only part of gaining access to the gold bullion of success; you must also have the gears properly aligned. And you must have sufficient willpower to turn the bolt that moves the locking pins back to get the door open.

We don't need all the pieces to get the full picture,
but we do require enough of the pieces

As a working adult, you most likely have come across some of the following concepts. You may have been told, "Just have faith and keep a positive attitude; it will all work out." Or, "Just make a decision and go!" Or, "Set your goals; that's all you need." These are all good piece parts to getting what you want, and they have their place in the cause and effect process, but as a full working system, they are incomplete. There are missing pieces of the puzzle. What you probably haven't seen is how these key gears align and interact with each other. They actually fit together and drive one another to create the outputs and occurrences you experience, and ultimately, they create your destiny.

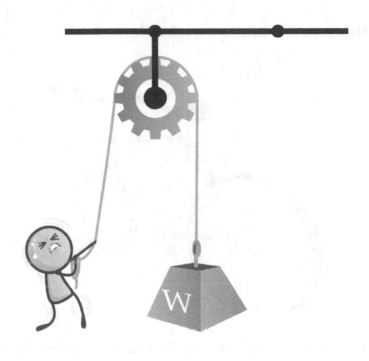

You need leverage; you need advantages

Leverage and advantages is what this book is about: giving you the best tools with a system engineered to maximize every advantage to reach your goals and objectives. Leverage is like money; there are different denominations. Some currencies have more power and influence than others. There are many other success factors beyond the 7 gears described in this book, but you will find that these are the "Big 7," the core elements that can make the biggest difference between success and failure. All references to leverage have to do with utilizing the key elements and factors between cause and effect.

Gears Need to be Placed and Aligned

If you had only one gear on your bike, imagine how limiting that would be. Depending on the gear ratio, it could be difficult to get started if, for example, the gear is too high. You'd have to get a running start and then jump on. Or maybe your one gear is so low that you pedal and pedal but just inch along, barely able to remain upright! Similarly, we need to have the *right gears* in the *right order* to maximize our power source into action and forward movement.

Without going any further, you could apply any one or two of these gears and be at an advantage. For example if you just applied **Gear 2, Operating System-Blueprint,** and **Gear 7, Action,** without any of the others, you would be two steps ahead of 90% of the population who do not set written, reviewed goals and do not take strategic action. But what if you could increase those two advantages even more? Starting today, you can, by learning and applying all 7 gears in the right order and sequence!

Two gears are better than one

In the world of radio communications, obtaining maximum transmitter output power requires a **tuning** of the different stages of the amplifier. **For any maximum transfer of energy, there needs to be alignment,** and the 7 Gears are no different in that regard. They must be aligned and engaged to work at maximum effectiveness.

It's been said that acting on just one sound idea can create a turning point that could mean the defining difference towards your success. Most quantum leaps happen just this way. I challenge you to take advantage of the synergistic combination of all 7 of these gears.

The combination is the key

When you look at any life-changing enhancements or discoveries in history, you find that it's the unique **combination** of materials, chemicals, or elements that creates a new innovation. For example, unintentionally weak glue on a small, colored paper tablet created the sticky note. And recently, an IBM research lab discovered "by mistake" a new synthetic polymer advancement not seen in 20 years. The new, strong recyclable material stands to revolutionize the plastics industry. As another example, researchers at Britain's University of Manchester have discovered what's been called the "first wonder material of the 21st century"—graphene. Graphene is 200 times stronger than steel, conducts heat and electricity, and has been tested to neutralize cancer stem cells. Beyond simply fulfilling a need, all great inventions involve a mixture of ideas, concepts or technologies. Developments such as concrete, steel, smart phones, wrist phones, trucks, boats, airplanes, and even yo-yos are all combinations of one material or technology with another. The big breakthroughs seem to follow a formula or combination, many times without the inventor's knowledge. You could call it a **recipe for success**. The old axiom, "The whole is greater than the sum of its parts," applies to the 7 Gears. Applied in the right order, these elements will create an amazing outcome. These 7 gears are **the difference that will make the difference** in your life if you use them.

Attention-Awareness

Energy streams where Attention beams

Thoughts and light are similar energy forms in that they can both be diffused or focused. Have you ever completed a presentation or engaged in intense discussion, and then later felt exhausted? It's not because of any major physical exertion, but because mental-emotional energy was drawn from you. Have you ever spent time with a negative person or entered into an argument, and later felt drained from the experience? Every day, we are processing a constant exchange of positive and negative energy.

Statistics report that we spend an inordinate amount of time focusing on the past. Do you really want to give that energy away to the past? Energy streams where attention beams. Light is frequency and energy. It is important to be mindful of the light of Attention and Awareness. This is what we mean when we say something "brings to light" or "sheds light on the subject of" something else. Imagine trying to play Ping-Pong in total darkness. You *might* hit the ball once. You need the light to see where things are, both physically and mentally.

The universe of energy operates by **exact laws and orderly principles**. Throughout the course of human history, we as a race of intelligent beings have made huge advances in industry, technology, mechanics, chemistry, medicine, new materials and designs, and more efficient production methods. Each successive discovery about how our universe works confirms that we live in an orderly universe and everything happens for a reason. All of the laws of nature are invisible, and the realm of the invisible—what's outside our limited range of senses—is much more powerful than the visible world. We can see and experience the effects. These causes are not limited to the physical universe, but include thoughts, ideas and beliefs. The famous verses, "According to your faith, be it unto you," and, "Whatsoever man sows, that shall he also reap," are not simply referencing physical actions. Sown seeds are *causes,* and the product of that seed is the *effect*. Seeds of jealousy, hate, bigotry, anger, and contempt all reap a result, an effect. And just as powerfully, "seed thoughts" of kindness, happiness, gratitude, friendliness, and love produce and multiply after their kind.

Your Stack of Chips

On the day you were born, you secured a place at the game table of life. You've been dealt a hand of life cards, just like Prince William, Oprah Winfrey, and Richard Branson have. Every waking day you are **playing your hand.** We've each been given the ability to think and reason. Some of our "life cards" can be changed out for better ones. But there's something else we were given at birth: time! If the cards we've been dealt are our opportunities, talents, gifts, good mind, body, and senses, then *time* is our stack of chips. Time, like a stack of chips, is limited, valuable, and can be spent, wasted, or lost. Time life chips can be invested wisely or foolishly, or even stolen. Making a play is taking a calculated risk. It means taking action with what you have, where you are. You want to collect as many advantage cards as you can, and working the 7 Gears is one of those advantages.

One of the primary purposes of the first six gears is to get you to the point of moving that 7th Gear and **taking organized, well-directed action.** Action, as you will see, is the primary point of power, but not the only point. Our life journey is not a flat surface, but rather a continuation of plateaus, of ups and downs. We all are on a roller coaster ride of good and bad, happy and unhappy, success and failure. In our life journey, we can have a smoother, more enjoyable ride if we have the best complement of tools and skills and the best mode of transportation.

Applying these 7 gears has had a profound effect on my life, and I want to share my findings with you. All of these important truths are an integral part of navigating your way forward to successful outcomes. These knowledge nuggets are potential power, but not power as a force *until* acted upon. **It's ACTION that gives you traction!** Action is the tangent point of POWER; it's where the rubber meets the road. In this book, you'll find out how this works to maximize the return on your efforts to get ahead.

To Get the Most out of this Book

- As you read through the concepts and ideas, keep an open mind; think from the perspective of, "how can I *use* this to my advantage?" We are all tuned into the **Station WIIFM: W**hat's **I**n **I**t **F**or **M**e? And something in this book will be transmitting on at least one channel that resonates with you.

- This book is packed with a lot of valuable information and ideas. Study the big picture as presented in Part One, and then dig into the details like a spiraling funnel.

- To get the exciting results you want, you have to CARE enough! And never let up on caring enough!

- When you come across a concept you've heard before, don't just gloss over it. Understand that it's the *combining* of one or more known ideas to another that can be the *eureka!* moment, the defining difference that changes the chemistry and direction of a thought. Associate any new concepts with what you already know.

- If this copy is a paper version, then underline, write notes and drawings all over it. Or if your e-reader has a highlighting feature, use it. Make it personal.

- To make the 7 Gears work in your life you must **apply** what you learn about them.

- Remain objective throughout the entire book.

- Be alert to even one new concept, idea, or perspective. Be open and ready for it. Reread certain sections that resonate with you. Go back to anything that grabbed your attention.

Core Beliefs Worth Adopting

- Everything happens with a cause behind it, and everything can be of value IF you view it as such.

- Successful people aren't born that way; they followed a certain path and process, and you can do it too.

- As within (the mental realm), so without (the physical realm). This is the Law of Correspondence.

- "Man was designed for accomplishment, engineered for success, and endowed with the seeds of greatness." -Zig Ziglar[4]

- Every one of your attitudes, beliefs and actions are 1) at your command, or 2) holding you hostage. It's your decision—always.

- You set your limitations; you set your path by default or by design.

- We have a responsibility to act on our talents, gifts and abilities, to make a contribution. Be on the lookout for finding and building on what you already know you have as a talent. Realize you DO have more than one talent.

- Your commitment and belief **must come first** before accomplishment. Success also depends on the support and cooperation of other people.

- Since we all share the same brain structure and mental faculties, what one has done, others can do also—this means YOU!

Commitments that Pay Huge Dividends

- COMMIT to being a **lifelong learner** dedicated to steady improvement in all eight goal areas (we will cover these in the 2nd Gear).

- COMMIT to **Sustained Unwavering Progress** through your *Daily Action Habits* **(SUPDAH)**. Make every moment count.

- COMMIT to applying the exercises. Step off the curb and into the parade. "Of all sad words of tongue or pen, the saddest are these, 'It might have been.'" -John Greenleaf Whittier

A Few Definitions

Here are definitions of a few of the metaphoric graphic symbols and emblematic references that will be used throughout this book.

GEAR – Dynamic interactive moving factor or principle. One of seven primary elements that cascade information and energy from the previous gear into the next one. Each gear adds and combines its own information and energy onto the next gear and integrates with the other gears bi-directionally. All 7 gears are systematically placed and aligned between the First *Cause* Gear and the *Effect* Gear.

COG® – A *traction factor* or important element essential to causing and transferring contact movement to any one of the gears. Also known as the teeth in a gear, or the tangent point of contact. Cog is also the character you will see throughout the book.

Cog

FIRST CAUSE – Source reasons primarily emanating from the Cause gears of all possibilities.

The **COLLABORATION CONTINUUM**® — A dynamic communications model depicting 7 personal and business relationship stages and levels. As the foundational factor in **effective communications** process, the Collaboration Continuum shows that your success depends on the support and cooperation of other people. Nobody is a solo act.

COGNO-KINETICS® — The integrated combination of *Cognitive* processing of perception, learning, reasoning (in psychology, philosophy, neuroscience and linguistics) with *Kinetic* principles of putting in motion, or supplying motive force, operating through a *Cybernetic* communication and control process as a system. The science behind *The 7 Gears Between Cause & Effect*.

SUPDAH® — A quick reference mnemonic standing for *Sustained Unwavering Progress* through *Daily Action Habit.*

MTA — Acronym for **Motivation To Action.**

PERFORM-O-STAT® — Represents the performance status level of your emotions and physical condition and set point, either turned up or down similar to a thermostat.

CAUSE

ANY
POSSIBILITY
INFINITE
POTENTIAL

PART ONE

CAUSE–*BE*–CAUSE

The Area of Any Possibility, Any Opportunity

"Cause and effect is as absolute and undeviating in the hidden realm of thought as in the world of visible and material things. Mind is the master weaver, both of the interior garment of character and the outer garment of circumstance."

– James Allen[5]

The Cause Side

The Law of Cause and Effect, also known as *causality,* has more than one philosophical path. The western traditional version traces back to Aristotle, who called out four kinds of cause: material cause, formal cause, efficient cause, and final cause. It is not the intent of this book to provide a history lesson on the varying philosophies of cause, but simply to work from the common definition of the law of cause and effect as the relation between a series of factors (causes) and a phenomenon (the effect). To use a modern-day reference that we can all relate to, Wikipedia tells us cause factors can take the form of objects, processes, properties, variables, facts, and states of affairs.

One Supply Source

Our Creator put this Universal Law of Cause and Effect in place, with the cause side containing three important factors:

1. It is the basis of **undeviating** truth.
2. It is the **starting place** reason behind all that happens.
3. **YOU can tap into it now,** because everything exists in the now.

For instance, the material to build a luxury jetliner has existed for thousands of years, just waiting for someone to come along and create something out of it. What we term "creation" is really discovery. It's the combination of unknown elements with what is already known that births a discovery. We have an inborn curiosity to learn, advance, grow, improve, and create. Our Creator has given us the material AND means to do all that. With such a gift, why wait passively for the next good idea? Why not be proactive and use the process to our advantage?

Tapping into the Cornucopia of Abundance

In order to tap into and transfer the energy and power contained in Causes, there must be sufficient alignment to transfer that energy into the form and direction needed to deliver the outcomes, results, and effects you're after. Like in the story of Aladdin's lamp, you must know the right "words" and say them in **the right combination**.

Having the right combination AND turning the handle
gets the opportunity door open

The source and composition of cause is the combination of intelligence AND energy. Energy is omniscient and omnipresent, and it cannot be created or destroyed, only changed in form and level. Energy can only be transferred from one form to another, such as when water changes from ice to steam vapor. Quantum science tells us matter is made of fast-moving subatomic particles with 99.9% space in between. If **everything has a vibrating frequency,** then so does the energy of attention and our thoughts!

Albert Einstein's famous $E=MC^2$ formula explains the relationship between mass and energy. And I believe there is intelligence behind energy and mass. There is an all-pervading infinite intelligence within the vast fluctuating energy field of Cause. Think about it: when it was proclaimed, "Let there be light," light became an energy form with intelligence behind it and within it. As co-creators, we have taken light energy and created many amazing things with it. And how is it that as a baby grows, its duplicating cells somehow "know" to start creating brain cells, then heart cells, etc.? At the cellular level, there is obviously an intelligence that directs living cells to duplicate from first conception.

The entire Universe of Cause and Effect is made up of varying forms and levels of energy. And as humans, we are able to tap into and be conduits of some of that energy. We are also recipients of any Effects whose paths we are in. Energy and matter are in a *constant transition* between visible and invisible states and back again, with thought processes interceding.

Other Forms of Source Energy Potential

One amazing example of the tremendous power of potential energy is found in one of earth's most basic substances, water. Scientists and researchers tell us that one gram of water contains the equivalent amount of energy of 20,000 tons (yes, *tons*) of exploding TNT! The USGS estimates that 96.5% of the earth's water is in the oceans, and one cubic mile of ocean = 1,100 trillion gallons of water. Now multiply that by 326,000,000 cubic miles! Keep in mind, this is just the water were talking about, not the entire earth mass! The earth itself has untold amounts of buried resources in oil, gas, and minerals.

Turning the Handle

If you want to open the door to all opportunity and potential, there are two parts. First, you must have **the right combination**, or the right order and sequence of factors. Second, you must **turn the handle**; in other words, apply and internalize what you've learned. This is one of those missing puzzle pieces: you have to turn the handle, *not just have the combination!*

As spiritual beings, we have God-given access to infinite possibilities and resources, and like miners, we must have the right equipment, tools and techniques to draw out and process those resources. Now here is the great human tragedy: **Most people do not tap their hidden potential**. Why? There are two main reasons. First, they don't know such possibilities exist. And second, they don't *believe* they have access to any more opportunity than what they can see right in front of them! That's what makes it "hidden." This book is all about showing you the exciting possibilities waiting for you RIGHT NOW!

Now here is the difference that's going to make the difference for you. If you *really, really* want to improve your outcomes and experiences, then <u>you must</u> <u>**internalize** and **implement** what you learn</u>. Go back and reread the last line. It's that important!

No Respecter of Persons

The most powerful forces are invisible, and we are under the influence and command of those forces. The moon's gravitational pull stabilizes earth's climate, creating an effect that maintains the seasons. As a powerful, invisible force, the moon's gravitational effect on earth works in tandem with the centrifugal force of the earth, creating tide changes on opposite sides of the planet.

Causes that impact us may not be pleasant or comfortable at times, but they are truthful. Real source causes never lie. When you decide to "get to the bottom of" something, you are getting to the truth, the reason behind it. And that's the hidden gem in gaining clear understanding of causes. They can serve you, or they can run your life. In this sense, causes are like money in the old adage, "Money makes a great servant and a terrible master." In his landmark work, *As a Man Thinketh*, James Allen assembles the best description of effects and circumstances. "Man is buffeted by circumstances so long as he believes himself to be the creature of outside conditions, but when he realizes that he is a creative power, and that he may command the hidden soil and seeds of his being out of which circumstances grow, he then becomes the rightful master of himself."[6]

First and Secondary Causes

There are two factors that influence outcomes and results, known as **primary** and **secondary causes**. A primary cause is a factor that *influences an effect* directly, without any interceding reasons. Secondary causes are unanticipated and unknown factors that intervene in what would have normally been a direct effect. These will be explained later with real life examples that will give you an added vantage point. One of my "eureka" moments was when I finally understood that **it's an inside job,** that any meaningful progress, improvement or favorable change starts from within. Like Dorothy's ruby slippers in the Wizard of Oz, the means to reach her goal was always there, waiting for the right time of discovery. Our ruby slipper is the ability to override our default mode of daily action habits and take control at any moment by first **deciding to**, which is one of the points of power.

Empowering

As the gear concept suggests, each gear acts as an element of our being. We are connected to the cause side at all times. We know this because we are constantly producing effects and results every day, if only by default or ignorance. The real power to seize control of most of our causes resides within us. How we think and process emotions internally is the difference that can make the difference in shaping the results and outcomes you're after. Understanding the placement and purpose of each of the 7 gears is the combination that opens the door to better outcomes and results. You'll have more control over life circumstances and a more advanced coping and handling skill set when bad things happen or when things aren't going your way.

It's time to shift your thinking if you really want to get into high gear!

February 15th Goal Setters

Statistics show that people who set New Year's fitness resolutions in January and head to the gym typically fall away about the middle of February. Habits are formed in the subconscious, which only recognizes a certain *recipe* of thought processes in order for lasting change to take hold. We will see that there is a way to break through this barrier, though, because the recipe is found in the 7 Gears!

One of the foundational requirements of activating the 7 Gears that lie between the CAUSE and EFFECT continuum is that to maximize transfer of power from one gear to another, gears must work in *harmony, resonance, and alignment*. All conditions, circumstances, and situations have origins that stem from some form of cause, either a primary cause or secondary mini-causes that add up to create a snowball of cumulative impact. If we focus our attention on **effects** to try to change our effects, it's like the scene in *Raiders of the Lost Ark* where they were digging in the wrong place. We need to focus on the causes! And all 7 gears are really cascading causes that add up to the Effect—your personal effects, outcomes, results and conditions. So let's go to work on each of those 7 critically important causes! Cause contains the element of truth, and **truth is light**. Lack of truth is darkness and ignorance. Let's not be kept in the dark.

Worth Remembering

- Cause contains the element of truth.

- It's been said, "Thoughts are causes, and conditions are the effects."

- Truth, like all Universal Laws, does not fade in and out or snap on and off. Like the sun, truth is always there, always ready for you as a lesson or a tool.

- Nature does not stray from her laws, which means you can trust them.

- You and I are here for a reason and a purpose.

- The application of our unique talents, skills, and abilities contributes to a cause greater than ourselves.

- Truth can hurt and be liberating. Truth is a corrective lens that sharpens your vision in all directions. Truth, once revealed, kills off the "bacteria" of lies and distorted thinking.

- Wisdom and truth are first cousins.

- Lasting change comes not with WHAT you think, but in HOW you think.

- Everything and everyone you come in contact with counts toward your growth.

- *Inner* space is the true final frontier.

- Summary: When the <u>Causes</u> change, then outcomes, results, and experiences (i.e., effects) change.

<u>Worth Doing</u>

- Be a part of a cause you believe in and *use* your talents, skill, and abilities. It must be something that resonates with your clearly defined purpose.

- *Practice* becoming more aware of your surroundings by looking more deeply at things, and you will realize your default perception is quite shallow.

- There isn't enough time to wallow in mediocrity and negative thinking. Exercise every waking moment's effort to avoid these robbers of the good life.

- If results are what counts, then let's identify what gets the best results.

PART TWO

The 7 GEARS
Between Cause and Effect

And now—the First Gear...

Gear · 1

ATTENTION-AWARENESS

"When you learn to pay attention, you create an opportunity to switch from passive to active awareness"

- Eric Allenbaugh[7]

CAUSE

The 1ˢᵗ Gear:

Your Knowledge-Transfer Medium

This first gear is the **first point of contact with Cause**; in other words, with all possibilities and opportunities. **Awareness** and **attention** are required to make each successive gear work. The realization of your goals and outcomes depends on your level of concentration on this gear. There are two forms of attention-awareness, *internal* and *external.*

It's been said that thought is the connecting link between the finite and the infinite. This is where the gear of **Attention-Awareness** comes in. It is in direct contact with the Cause, with infinite possibilities. Whenever we take a closer look at any universal principles or laws, we discover there are elements and factors governing their operation that are not readily observed on a surface level. Most of the dynamic factors within the seven gears are just that—invisible, hidden, yet very powerful and at constant work in manifesting tangible, physical effects, outcomes, and results. This first gear, like all the gears you'll be reading about, has both a direct and indirect influence on your outcomes and results.

One of my favorite romantic comedies, *Joe Versus the Volcano,* provides an excellent portrayal of one man's search for his life's meaning and significance. Hypochondriac Joe Banks, played by Tom Hanks, is allegedly diagnosed with an incurable disease, with only months to live. He is approached by a wealthy businessman with a life-changing opportunity. With nothing to lose, he agrees to an all-expense-paid trip, leaving his miserable East Coast job to travel across the world to a South Pacific island, where he willingly jumps into a smoldering volcano to appease the volcano god. On the journey, he encounters three Meg Ryan characters, the third of which is the troubled daughter of the wealthy businessman. Ryan, as Patricia, is tasked with taking him in her yacht to his destination island. A peaceful evening finds them lying on the deck looking up at the stars. Patricia tells Joe that her father believes most of the world is asleep and that only a few are awake and aware. It's true that most of us are so caught up in the hustle and bustle of moment-to-moment activities that we lose sight or awareness of the deeper things in life.

Sensory Acuity

In the animal kingdom, keen depth and level perception mean survival. Amazingly, each creature, whether it swims, flies, runs or crawls, has unique sensory capabilities. Most are superior to human senses. Eagles and hawks have eyesight that is 3–4 times sharper than human eyesight, and sharks can detect electrical fields from distant fish, even if they're hiding!

Most people never really get to experience their full potential. Sadly, most people do indeed "go to the grave with [their] song still in them," as Thoreau wrote. How sad that millions of epitaphs should read, "Died at age 40–Buried at age 70." The point of this is that you may have lost sight or not realized the REAL depth and value of your possessions. You have an amazing tool that's been given to work with **Attention-Awareness (Decision**, Gear 6)! But for now, just know that you have gifts waiting to be unwrapped!

When our awareness expands or changes on any subject area, the world around us changes for better or for worse. As the first gear, Awareness is the first influencing factor that causes the changes to all the other gears. Attention and Awareness are like mountain streams that start the cascading effect, leading to the great river of outcomes and consequences downstream. Each successive gear has a multiplying influence that drives the Action Gear, which then delivers outcomes and results, either positive or negative. To learn of a *truth* or cause or reason is enlightening; to learn of an *untruth* or something that "just isn't so!" can be just as enlightening.

Awareness Is a Type of Vision

Awareness is a type of vision in that what you *see* is what you're aware of, and what you don't see is out of your sight range, or it's not clear. In physical vision, we know that people can be nearsighted or farsighted, and with corrective lenses are able to see both far and near.

We Are Co-Creators

There is something inherent inside each of us that urges us to grow, expand, improve, and learn. Otherwise, we would still be living our lives like our ancestors did thousands of years ago, with no improvements, just as birds build nests the same today as they did eons ago. If necessity is the mother of invention, then dissatisfaction is the father. Inspired dissatisfaction is a good thing when it drives us to improve.

Is it some great coincidence that of all the planets in our solar system and beyond, only this one planet has all the resources needed for us to build a rocket to go to Mars? We build jets, space stations, roads, bridges, skyscrapers, and cell phones. All the energy and elements have been here for perhaps millions of years, ready and waiting! It is no accident that we have what are called **higher faculties of mind given to us as tools to explore, invent, create, advance, and improve our current life conditions.**

The Six Higher Faculties of the Human Mind

The dictionary defines faculty as "an inherent power or ability." I believe they are both powers and abilities. So what are these faculties? Just as the 7 Gears are a set of factors, the six higher faculties of the human mind are previously known factors. We all know of them as individual things. The big difference, however, is in realizing how important they are to your success and wellbeing. Like working a muscle for strength and fitness, exercising these faculties can step up your power and abilities to supercharge your 7 gears. That means discovering hidden possibilities waiting for you that you'd otherwise never know. Let's take a look at these six high-level faculties.

Memory — It's been said that memory is the art of attention. "There is no such thing as a 'bad' memory - only a trained or untrained memory," says memory master William Hersey.[8] Everyone thinks in pictures. Imagination and memory work together as they use our internal vision, our inner eye. There is a whole science and art to exercising memory. Many tools and techniques are available to enhance and improve your memory, and most of them are fun as games. Get some of the memory apps on your smart phone or tablet. It's worth the exercise, as you are sharpening an important ability.

Reason — This capability is our capacity for logical, rational, analytic thought, to form conclusions based on facts presented, and it is thought to be intelligence, be it emotional or mental. This is another factor that separates us from the animal kingdom.

Perception – This ties in with this first Gear of Attention-Awareness because it's a consciousness that recognizes and interprets sensory stimuli. It also works in tandem with memory as a reference point to neurological processing. Additionally, perception ability is a component of **Gear 4 (Perspective-Viewpoint)**.

Intuition – There are some who believe intuition should not be confused with "sixth sense." I believe they are tied together. Intuition can be described as a hunch, knowing or sensing something outside of rational realms, or an impression or belief obtained neither by perception or reason.

Will – Will is used when you deliberately choose a specific course of action. It's a resolve with a certain level of determination. A lot of people become jaded when hearing about the long-term effects of willpower and how weak it seems to be when *relying on it alone* as a sole source motivator. How many New Years' resolutions have you kept this year based on willpower alone? This factor ties in with Gear 6, Decision–Choice. You will see later on how Gears 3, 4, and 5 must be running strong in order to generate lasting willpower that works.

Imagination – This faculty is one of the biggies. It is the power to generate images both still and moving, but it can be more than images. You have the ability to generate full sensory-rich mental experiences. You can, for example, imagine being at a party in your honor, the sound of champagne glasses clinking, the wafting scents of hors d'oeuvres and perfume, laughter and conversation, etc. What we forget is that the power and impact of imagination can be used constructively or destructively. Again, this faculty has great impact on all 7 gears.

Every invention, advancement, or idea is always *first* imagined. When you imagine *as if* it's true or real, you put your foot in the door of infinite possibilities!

All of these tools are special endowments that are meant to be used. We also need to keep them in good running order through use and exercise, and they should never be allowed to atrophy through neglect. They need to stay sharp and well lubricated through intentional use. The rewards will be worth it; they are the grease that makes the gears run smoothly and effectively.

"The ultimate value of life depends upon awareness and the power of contemplation rather than upon mere survival."

- Aristotle[9]

5 SENSES

6TH SENSE

Two Levels of Awareness

There are two forms of awareness:

INTERNAL — Thoughts, Feelings, Ideas, Insight Flashes

EXTERNAL — Tangible, Visible, External, Outside World

Both internal and external awareness are THOUGHT and ENERGY forms, and both are magnetic in nature. Focused attention on anything begins to pull *more of the same,* whether it's internal or external. Energy streams where attention beams.

Additionally there are **two levels and directions** of awareness and attention. The internal has been described as our 6th sense, that inner sense of knowing, while external awareness depends on our five physical senses of sight, sound, touch, taste, and smell. All of our senses are bi-directional in nature. For example, you can look out into the physical world (external attention) and see a purple flowering tree. You can hear its rustling leaves and catch a whiff of its scent. But you could also use your internal attention to imagine a sensory-rich vision of the same thing while sitting at your desk.

The 6th sense points internally as mental, spiritual self-awareness and as a sort of channel detector. One of the popular TV shows in the mid-1960s was called "The Man From U.N.C.L.E.," a James Bond-type series. The two lead spies had special communication pens. They would pull out their pens and say, "Open Channel D!" Our 6th sense is a sort of "channel D" in that it receives special signals that can sense or "D"-tect danger or auras of cold or warmth in a room of people. Have you ever walked into a party or business meeting and sensed a chill? You could just feel it! Another characteristic of these senses is that they work quickly, nearly instantaneously.

Waiting in the dentist's office was always nerve-wracking for me as a kid. When I was a youngster, they always had a popular kids' magazine called *Highlights*. It was always fun to go to the hidden pictures section. The game was to find all the hidden images disguised in the main picture: Look for the upside down turtle, a hammer, an oak leaf, etc. This focused my attention on finding the images, and it also worked to temporarily take *attention* off the terror of being in the dentist's office! If your *interest* is focused on looking for something, you usually find it! This is how our attention–awareness can be focused or steered to anything of a positive nature that is valuable and empowering. It can just as easily focus on something disempowering if you're "looking" for trouble through a negative thought image. You'll start drawing more trouble until you change the direction of your attention. Just as the sun's rays, when focused and steady, begin to produce heat (think of a small boy frying an ant with a magnifying glass), focusing our attention on something bad for too long will begin to pull us down, or worse, paralyze our ability to act.

Opportunity Awareness

You need to be home when opportunity comes knocking!

If your sensory acuity is distracted, you can be in the right place at the right time, but still miss the opportunity. You must be AWARE of the potential opportunity at the right time. Haven't you ever looked back on a time in your life when you could have taken advantage of great opportunity but didn't, because your attention-awareness level was pointed in a different direction at the time? Opportunities are like ships sailing to and fro in the harbor, and you can **never wait** for your ship to come in! You must get in your dinghy and start rowing out to where *opportunity boats* are running! And even if you get out to where the boats are and can't get aboard one, just being in the shipping lanes puts you at an advantage for the next one that comes along. Today, there is no lack of opportunity; in fact, there is more opportunity now than ever before in history. Business trends and emerging technologies, combined with growing problems and challenges, are like a fantastic pearl bed awaiting discovery.

Imagination and Awareness

Awareness of an opportunity requires the imagination to consider all its possibilities. You are about to gain a new awareness of how the 7 gears interoperate and support each other to work as tools that will draw out your full potential and manifest into the physical world of outcomes, results and conditions.

"ATTENTION! May I Have Your Attention?"

Or

"Hey, Watch Where You Point That Thing!"

Many people don't have a clear idea of how the human mind works. We're not talking about the brain here; we're talking about the mind as *thought process*. The brain contains a miraculous network of synaptic nerve functions that carry electrical impulses with incredible speed and complexity. The mind generates over 50,000 thoughts a day, but 98% of those thoughts are focused on something in the past. And researchers have identified that the average person's attention wanders every 6–10 seconds per minute. You may have been told to "get control of your faculties." Well, just what does that mean, and how is it relevant to this first gear of attention-awareness?

As author Bob Proctor suggests in many of his talks, your results are an expression of your awareness. That viewpoint plays an important part in this first gear called

Attention-Awareness. Attention has inner energy, and *focus* sharpens that energetic force just as a laser is focused light energy. Attention power is strengthened through practice, through being aware of your awareness.

There is a section of the human brain called the reticular activating system that, in addition to regulating sleep-wake functions, causes our level of attention to sharpen and focus. As you will see when we get to **Gear 2, Operating System,** this can be used to your advantage when your values, purpose and goals are sharp and strong. Developing keen, acute depth and level perception is the goal. Author Genevieve Behrend explains in her book *Your Invisible Power*,

> While the laws of the Universe cannot be altered, they can be made to work under specific conditions, thereby producing results for individual advancement, which cannot be obtained under the spontaneous working of the law by nature.[10]

Self-Awareness

The great Greek philosopher, Socrates (469-399 BC) said, "Know thyself." We are complex, unique spiritual beings in physical bodies with mental and emotional capabilities wrapped in a personality. You could say God "broke the mold" in creating each one of us, not just a select few. For each one of these characteristics, we can be self-aware. We can, for example, be emotionally aware of how feelings work and function. We can gain spiritual awareness through religious texts and philosophical studies, through prayer and meditation. We can study the intricacies of the human body through studying health and fitness. All of these levels of self-awareness run through one or more of the six senses. The better we know ourselves, the better we can make improvements. We can make wiser decisions about what fits us best, such as a career path, and we can tap into inherent talents and capabilities that would otherwise lie dormant.

69

Think back to the scope and level of awareness you had during childhood, and then how your range of awareness expanded as a teenager. It grew from focusing on toys to boyfriends and girlfriends, then on to college and career paths. Your awareness should always be expanding so that when opportunities present themselves, you're ready. One of the best ways to expand opportunity is in perfecting how you communicate with others. All opportunities have people attached to them.

Attention on Others—How to Expand Your Influence: The Secret of Charisma

We've all experienced the dynamic, energetic effect charismatic people seem to emit. Charisma is not a quality reserved for the rich and famous or for a select few. Because it's a personality trait, it can be developed. Researchers on the subject have identified common characteristics of those who radiate charisma. In particular, **Gears 1, 2, 3** and **5** contain elements of charisma when applied. **Gear 1** is pointing **Attention** away from yourself with the sensory acuity to read others' feedback, just as a good comedian reads his or her audience. Add to that the factors we will learn about in other gears--emotional resonance, clearly defined values, and a strong belief system—and this will produce a high-level mixture of love, passion and conviction that creates an irresistibly magnetic drawing power. Once internalized, the combined energy of all these factors creates a personal power that can expand your influence for good. Martin Luther King, Jr., Billy Graham, Franklin Roosevelt, and Mother Teresa are supreme examples of people who have demonstrated positive influence and charisma. No less important are the teachers, athletes, and business leaders who, through their passion, are just as influential and charismatic. Hopefully you've known someone who has had a positive impact on your life.

Conflict between the Conscious and Subconscious

As odd as it may sound, we need to be aware of our awareness, to be mindful of its importance. Awareness is not something you get; awareness is something you direct. Because awareness is always on when we are awake, it's a matter of what we are focusing on. Like a flashlight in a dark room, it's always pointing in one direction or another.

One of the things I tried to engrain in my kids was the mantra, "Pay attention; be alert; think ahead!" My hope was that it would program into them the importance of paying attention, whether crossing the street as young children or driving on the highway as teenagers. Attention is energy; it's like a light beam that can be diffused and scattered, or focused and increased all the way to laser-level intensity, a power which can cut through steel. Because focused attention is a skill and ability, it can be strengthened and improved through practice and persistence. If you spread your attention, your action gear to accomplishment dwindles. But when your awareness and attention are focused with clear intent—look out!

The Magnifying Glass—Concentration

Clarity with acute depth and level perception is the power of FOCUS.

For example, many of today's cars have a clear plastic lens cover that encases the headlights. Over time, they become cloudy and hazy because of weather and the effects of exposure to the sun's damaging UV rays. This causes headlights to lose focus and clarity because the lens becomes opaque. When our attention and focus are scattered, they become opaque and lose intensity and clarity.

71

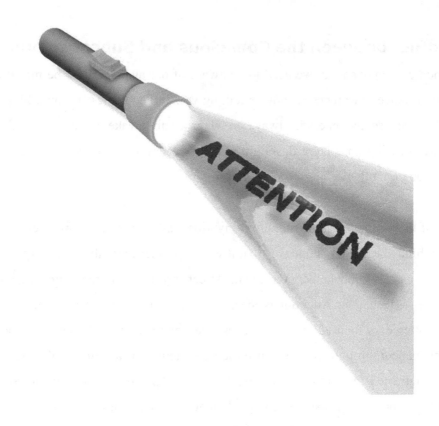

"*But everything exposed by the light becomes visible, and everything that is illuminated becomes a light.*"

(Eph. 5:13)[11]

The Light of Attention

One of the challenges of Attention energy and focus is **where** we point it. Is it pointed at what we don't want, or what we DO want? Often we are not "aware" (pun) of what we are focusing on and its debilitating effects. We can become habitual about what we focus on! If we focus on something negative, then more negative thoughts will start collecting like metal shavings to a magnet. Who are you listening to: television, talk radio, comedians, YouTube gag reels, and pessimistic co-workers? Some people justify this by saying, "Well, I need to be informed." I wouldn't challenge that except when it overrides your ability to think and reason in a way that helps you to fulfill your purpose and goals. Insightful "eureka" moments rarely come to you during the New Year's Eve party.

Darkness hinders our ability to see, but there can be other blockades to clear sight as well. How different would bowling be if you had a sheet or curtain in front of the pins you were trying to knock down? In determining what to focus on, that "sheet" can show up in the form of your attitude or perspective.

RAS—Reticular Activating System

As mentioned earlier, there is a part of the brain labeled by neurologists as a "reticular formation" or system. This neural network of fibrous connections performs many functions. One of those functions includes affecting various levels of conscious awareness ranging from high alert attention and focus to the transitional sleep state. It also filters awareness on what we, by our own programming, define as important matters, and it deletes unnecessary information, again by our own programming. In other words, we pay attention to what is important to us.

For example, you buy a new Ford Model X, and what will you start seeing around town, especially if it's the same color? Every model X that is within your visual range! This is significant because it gives us a clue into how our mind works when intentions we deem important are revealed and filtered accordingly.

If you don't take the helm or steering wheel of attention and purposely direct it, you will drop back into default mode. The energy of attention can therefore be focused and directed to our benefit and goals, and it is a key factor in doing what you **do** want, not what you don't want. Opportunities that are valuable to you start showing up. It is not coincidence; it's putting your mind to work for you.

Uncle Lloyd's Ranch

When I was a kid growing up in Colorado, my mom and dad would make the trek up to Grandma Putnam's South Dakota ranch to celebrate the Thanksgiving holiday. After dinner at the homestead ranch house, my Uncle Lloyd would have my cousins George, John, and Cindy go with me to feed the cows with alfalfa, which we would load up from stacks into the back of his pickup truck. I was the hired hand for the week. If you've ever been to the southwestern corner of South Dakota, you know it's mostly flat. With about 20 hay bales loaded into the back of the truck, we would head out to where the cows were. Uncle Lloyd would put the pickup in "granny" gear (low first), and we would all jump out of the cab and into the back and start throwing the bales to the herd. The truck meandered along with no one at the wheel! And it worked really well because everyone was getting the bales out and Uncle Lloyd knew the terrain ahead.

However, when it comes to human attention, we must keep direction and control because we don't always know what the terrain ahead will be. Time is too precious and fast moving to be like a cork bobbing on the water, just drifting wherever the current goes. Focus and control are mental habits that demand vigilance. As the saying goes, "If you don't know where you're going, you'll end up somewhere else."

The GPS-EGS Analogy

As human communicators, we are immersed in a global communications system, or **Emotional Guidance Signal system** of sorts. For example, you think about someone that you haven't thought about for months or years, and just then the phone rings out of the blue. Well just what is "The Blue?" Your thought is the subject-info, and your emotions are the signal generator and receiver. Every kind of invisible signal wave is permeating through us, around us, into and out of us.

We are surrounded by a spectrum of frequencies and channels with a tiny sliver within our limited sensory range. If you've ever looked out on a lake or the ocean, you have glimpsed frequencies in constant motion displayed by ripples, waves and cross-currents.

Another Awareness Level

Have you ever walked into a room and gotten an immediate "feel" that was either good or bad, or a sense of happiness or sadness? The term "vibe" is actually quite accurate. We are all sending and receiving frequencies of feeling. We all have God-given "psychic-type" abilities, and we've all experienced it to some degree. It's important to realize that you have a powerful guide that is always with you and ready to serve. Its presence is merely a matter of degree, usage and trust. It can and should be exercised to improve its effectiveness. A skill most successful business leaders have in common is a highly developed faculty of the 6th sense—intuition. They all listen to their intuition or gut instinct, which in turn influences their decisions, Gear 6. As with any skill, you must make a conscious effort to exercise and respect your 6th sense as a special guide. The 6th sense, as it's been called, is too valuable a faculty to simply slough off as something that's just, "interesting." When you're being honest and open, without judgmental bias in your deeper thinking, you're *tapping into truth*. Moreover, it can keep your direction **compass needle** true and straight without being drawn off by "metallic" interference. That is why you will find it rare to discover in retrospect that your gut feeling was off.

*Your **True North Values Compass** always knows the way*

Conscious Mind

Your conscious thought processing is the lubrication that runs through all the gears. *All of the 7 gears are important and critical factors to achievement.* You will see how the conscious mind sparks the first point of power when it exercises decision making as Gear 6. The conscious mind is the energy conduit that puts life into all the gears. Ultimately, **it's all about taking action,** the right action to get the results and outcomes you want. The function and purpose of the first six gears is to get your conscious mind to turn that last gear, action. Attempting to make lasting change in habits, or sustained goal-reaching progress most often doesn't work at the conscious mind level. A dandelion weed will continue to grow if you only remove the top parts; you must get at the roots.

Subconscious Mind

*"Until you make the unconscious conscious,
it will direct your life and you will call it fate."*

- Carl Jung

The subconscious is said to be immeasurable in capability and function, and for good reason, since it's known to house all memories of your every living moment. It also directs body functions such as your heartbeat, fluid chemistry, digestion, injury healing, and baby making. Where does the intelligence come from that heals a broken leg or a cut finger? The mind never forgets and like film, it records everything and stores every memory and experience. Yes, our ability to recall to conscious thought level is blunted, but it's all there in our supercomputer hard drive subconscious. The human computer system *never shuts down.* Because the subconscious is considered to be central to our functioning existence, volumes have been written on the subject. New discoveries of its miracle-working powers and capabilities surface every year. The important point for the sake of this discussion is to follow author Joseph Murphy's advice in his book *The Power of Your Subconscious Mind* when he says, "Begin now to take care of your conscious mind, knowing in your heart and soul that your subconscious mind is always expressing, reproducing, and manifesting according to your habitual thinking."[12] Your subconscious mind doesn't evaluate what's good or bad for you; it takes orders that you give it through long-held mental pictures that are charged with intense emotion. *Emotionally charged mental pictures are the dialect the subconscious understands and acts on.*

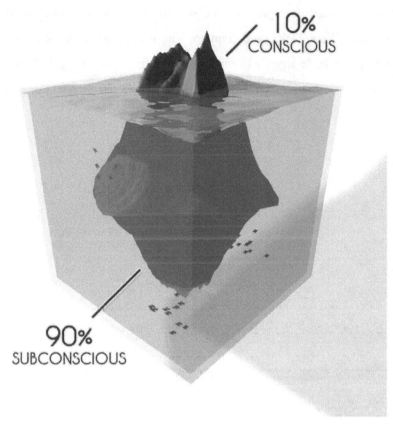

10%
CONSCIOUS

90%
SUBCONSCIOUS

Common analogy of the conscious and subconscious mind

The subconscious is often portrayed as that portion of ice in the iceberg below the water, the other 90% that is deeper and more powerful than the 10% above the water. Think of this iceberg as your individual mind and the vast ocean of water it's floating in as a universal consciousness. They are both made of the same material, and the universal consciousness is omnipresent, always there. The ocean water is always in contact with us. Wherever you step into the ocean, you're in contact with and a part of all the continuous water on the planet. Whether you're in San Diego, Tokyo, Dublin, or Auckland, you're still connected and a part of it. It's the same for the huge spectrum ocean of invisible frequency-vibration. The water in this example represents the spectrum of the 5 brainwave frequencies: Alpha, Beta, Theta, Delta, and Gamma. The human brain broadcasts micro-level electrical pulse code signals in the following frequency ranges. Measured by an electroencephalograph machine (EEG), brainwaves transmit in these ranges.

Levels of Consciousness

Channel Frequencies of Awareness

Each "channel" frequency influences our mental health. This block of frequencies serves as an integral component to our **Cogno-Kinetic** health and wellbeing. Scientists refer to them as "neural oscillations," and they are active all through our central nervous system. Similar to a radio channel, they also generate properties of amplitude and phase. It's the synchronization of these neural structures running as a sort of bio-fiber-optic microprocessor that is the science behind Cogno-Kinetics. These synchronized neural oscillations are connected to a number of cognitive functions such as motor control, memory, awareness-perception, and transfer of information. Incredible as it sounds, our planet earth has its own resonant frequency known as Schumann resonance, which occurs at approximately 7.83 Hz.

Here are those frequency channels:

(Hertz is a measure of cycles per second. 14Hz = 14 cycles per second.)

Beta – (12–40 Hz) The fully awake conscious state where we think and reason. Stress and angst can run through this frequency.

Alpha – (8–14 Hz) Relaxation daydreams, light meditation, also known as the gateway channel to the subconscious, most conducive to visualization, imagination.

Theta – (4–7 Hz) Sleeping and light meditation—the transitional sleep state; Spiritual connection—very deep relaxation level, yet conscious.

Delta – (1–4 Hz) Deepest sleep state, unconscious range.

Gamma – (30 -70 Hz+) Cognitive functioning, including learning and memory, insights, binding senses of perception, focus, intuition, creativity.

"If you want to find the secrets of the universe, think in terms of energy, frequency and vibration."

- Nikola Tesla

There must be a collaboration of the conscious and subconscious to *enforce* and *sustain* the inner power of both mind levels. It's important to gain a basic understanding of these key discoveries about the conscious and subconscious mind. Researchers and psychologists will tell you that when the left brain right brain work *interdependently,* the conscious and subconscious are unified such that theta brain waves increase. This symbiotic state is believed to be the spawning ground for works of genius in music, literary creations and great technological inventions.

Additionally psychologists and mind science researchers have discovered these characteristics:

1) The subconscious mind works like a "servo-mechanism" that only takes orders and goes to work to deliver what you put on the menu. As an order taker, the subconscious only takes commands as **"make it happen"** orders.

2) It does not recognize or respond to the word "no." Every thought command is a *yes order*. It will act to deliver *positive* or *negative* thought pattern **equally**. This is why you must guard your thinking.

3) We all have beliefs running in our subconscious mental core that drive every behavior.

4) The subconscious does **not** know the difference between real or imagined thought pictures. This is significant because it explains how we can get

conflicting intentions in our outward experiences because of inward cross wiring or disharmony between the two levels.

5) We can be sending conflicting message orders without consciously being aware of what we're doing!

6) One more operating factor about the subconscious is that it is very "emo"— that is, it responds to intense emotions. Thought patterns that are laced with **intense feeling,** happy or unhappy, positive or negative *get through* and are taken as, *"this is what I want!"* The subconscious delivers according to the intensity-induced compelling command it receives.

One way to maximize the effectiveness of your subconscious going to work for you and not against you is to ***sell* the outcome** you desire **as *already* here.** You've got to, at some level, believe it. A thought repeated enough times becomes a pattern, and thought patterns combined with a high level of *emotion* get the green light into the subconscious mind. Call it your internal program or operating system. As you can see, you can upgrade your mind software to eliminate "bugs" and improve your mental and emotional performance! Since we exist as triune mental-spiritual-physical beings, all three functions are upgraded.

The degree of conscious-subconscious harmony indicates the level of mental, emotional and physical health and wellbeing. It is believed in some circles that the consciousness of mankind is capable of nearly unlimited expansion and that the mental awareness of humanity was not meant to be 90 percent "underwater."

The Transitional Sleep State

The conscious and subconscious mind have a transitional zone much like the locks in the Panama Canal that separate the Atlantic from the Pacific. Called by many names, it reminds me of the green-tinted door guard in the City of Oz. You don't just walk in. The guard cries, "Not no body! Not no how!"[13] And yet the *password* to the subconscious "city" is essential if you are to gain control override. This is where the seat of habit-formed programming resides. It's also where our deep-seated emotional belief systems reside. To make lasting changes, you must get through to the subconscious mind level.

Placement and Position of the 7 Gears

- **Mental/Emotional/Internal—Below the line**
- **Physical/Visible/External—Above the line**

The Invisible Power of Awareness and Attention

There are some challenges that can impede your ability to move forward.

For example, my home football team, the Denver Broncos ("GO Broncos!" I was programmed to say that!), has quarterback Peyton Manning, who is at the time of this writing at the top of his game and is considered one of the best quarterbacks of all time. Manning has developed the skill of keen, acute depth and level perception that can read the opposing team's defense moves in micro seconds and adjust the next play accordingly. Good business leaders also have this ability to read their "defense" (competition or customer base) quickly. Wal-Mart does this electronically for every transaction, every second around the world, giving the company instant buying trend information.

Like images seen through night vision goggles, unseen opportunities flash into view as "aha" moments

Level and Direction of Awareness

- Internal 6th Sense (Mental/Spiritual)
- External 5 Senses (Physical/Outward)

Everyone Cycles through These Levels of Awareness Every Day:

- **Unconscious incompetence:** You don't know you don't know.
- **Conscious incompetence:** You know you don't know.
- **Conscious competence:** You know that you do know.
- **Unconscious competence**: You know and you don't have to think about it; it's automatic, such as driving to work or riding a bike.

Awareness is the pathway to gaining knowledge. The old axiom, "Knowledge is power," is true but incomplete in that knowledge not applied is like having a 400-horsepower engine that stays in neutral. You can rev the engine all day, but until you *engage the gears* nothing happens.

Attention Diversions

Most people are focused on external things primarily because that's what's in front of them. Think of the distracting potential of the Internet. Staying on task can be difficult because of the temptation to click on a story or an eye-catching byline. Have you ever been sitting in front of your computer doing legitimate work and gotten pulled away by some flashing ad or viral video, and then before you know it, an hour has gone by? What happened? **Diversion**. In addition to television, we now have at our fingertips more hi-tech ways to communicate and interact than ever before with the booming use of social media such as Facebook, Twitter, Viber and more to come. These are not bad things except that overuse of these great tools can consume your valuable time and build distraction and diversion that cause delays in reaching your goals.

Direction of Attention

Thinking from a multidimensional perspective, we not only operate from different levels of awareness, we think in different directions and always **one way at a time!** Like the flashlight in a dark room, attention points in one direction at a time. We will see later how questions shape and point our attention and focus. Asking the right kind of question can do wonders in changing our attention from negative to positive. It also is one of the keys to accessing the Cause Gear of any possibility.

Power Level of Awareness

There is yet another aspect of Awareness and Attention. Attention-Awareness has a **power level**. Think of the analogy of "shedding light" on a subject. Light is **a form of energy** just like the sun. And when attention is focused with enough power behind it, you've got something that can make things happen! When you activate and sustain laser-like focus, things get done and time seems to warp. Concentration is vital to so-called mind power and is a key element in converting mediocrity into high achievement.

Because our attention gets pulled and pointed in hundreds of directions every day, it becomes easy to forget that we always have the ability to control our attention, our minds. What you focus on immediately begins to influence your emotions either positively or negatively. Cartoonist and journalist James Thurber (1894-1961) said, "Let us not look back in anger, nor forward in fear, but around in awareness."[14]

State of Consciousness

In the book *The Power of Awareness*, author Neville Goddard offers an attention-strengthening exercise to do just before going to sleep at night. He instructs readers to recall every activity of the day in reverse order. Just as working a muscle of the body builds its strength, so does exercising your attention. Goddard says, "All progress depends on an increase of attention," and that "the power of your attention is the measure of your inner force."[15] This exercise is really an exercise in memory enhancement. With today's thousands of apps for anything and everything, there are apps that are designed to test and improve your memory. I recommend adding to your smart phone or laptop some memory recall and attention exercising games.

Since the underlying theme in this book is about seizing your best opportunities and improving your outcomes and life conditions, you will see a number of change factors presented in different ways and from different angles. Changing your consciousness is essential if you're serious about making changes in your physical results world. Actually, all of the first five gears have an inherent element of consciousness change leading up to taking the right action, the kind of action that is pointed in the right direction, your direction.

You need more than one gear to get up the hill

A few years back I had a contract-consulting job in San Diego and was living in a hotel-apartment on Shelter Island. The hotel offered 1950s-style one-speed bicycles to ride around the island for fun. They worked great because the land was flat, but to use those one-speed bikes in the hills would be extremely difficult. We navigate through life in much the same way, through a lot of ups and downs, hills and curves. We need more than one gear to keep moving to adjust to the landscape up ahead. The information in this chapter alone is enough to make a difference in your life for the better if you apply and integrate it into what you've already learned as a life student. Having **more than one gear** to get up and down life's hills and valleys applies to having the tools, techniques, program method, and belief systems. It means using your 7 gears systematically.

Many people just aren't aware of the links between Cause and Effect. Nor do they understand the importance of the gears. We all need to **discover** our resources and powers within so that we can **leverage** them to make the most of ourselves. But how else can we best learn to transfer that power into an efficient machine that moves us forward with minimum loss of power transfer? We can do this by systematically activating and aligning the 7 gears.

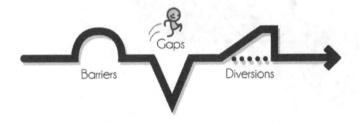

Did Dave Thomas, Ray Croc, Donald Trump, Michael Dell, Steve Jobs, Sergey Brin, and Larry Page just accidentally build successful businesses? Did Sir Hillary and 2000 mountain climbers thereafter just show up on the top of Mt. Everest? Or is there really something to organized thought process and doing things in a certain way? Is there a formula, a recipe that can give you more exciting experiences and outcomes?

Worth Remembering

- Attention is a form of energy, as light, and can be focused and directed.

- What you focus your attention on has a drawing magnetic effect and draws more to itself.

- You must change your thoughts first to change your outcomes and results.

- Attention-Awareness has six input pathways –one internal and five external.

- The more you sharpen your sensory acuity, the more you eliminate unnecessary grief and frustration.

- Your Attention-Awareness Gear is the conduit to flash ideas and life changing "aha" moments.

- Your Attention-Awareness acuity is the *first point of contact* to the invisible energy power of all reasons, ideas, knowledge, and possibilities.

- Attention-Awareness is a prerequisite to the next six gears.

- The light of attention may be missing the opportunity in the dark because the beam is too weak or pointed in the wrong direction.

- **Summary: When your <u>Attention-Awareness</u> changes, your outcomes and experiences change.**

<u>Worth Doing</u>

- **Make a conscious daily effort to trust and exercise your 6th sense and intuition, and it will serve you well.**

- **Exercise putting your full attention on what you *DO* want, not what you don't want.**

- **When you exercise your imagination by intentionally focusing on any possibility, you're tapping into the Cause gear.**

- **Make sure you're home when opportunity comes knocking.**

- **Mental power is not something you *go get* because it's already in you, but you *must* make a conscious effort to draw it up and use it every day.**

- **At night, recall the day's events in reverse order as a mental exercise.**

- **Practice pointing your *Attention beam* away from fear and failure and on what you really want. This is a daily practice worth building.**

- Practice sharpening your *Attention-Awareness* by <u>looking deeper</u> in every direction. You'll be amazed at what you've been missing.

- When you become aware of an opportunity, you then have a short time to act on it or lose it forever.

- None of us is a solo act. We function better as pilot and co-pilot. Who have you chosen as your co-pilot?

We now shift into Second Gear,

which is...

Gear •2

OPERATING SYSTEM-BLUEPRINT

"Men are anxious to improve their circumstances, but are unwilling to improve themselves, and therefore remain bound."

- James Allen[16]

What is an Operating System-Blueprint?

All existence is made up of systems: the solar system, the earth's ecosystem, government systems, our cardiovascular system, railroad systems, refrigeration systems, and computer systems, to name a few. Within a computer is the core foundational program on which all other programs run and depend. Wikipedia defines the operating system as a collection of software that manages hardware resources and provides common services for computer programs. It works as an essential component of the system software.

Operating systems provide a software platform on top of which many additional programs can run as applications. The application programs are specific to the operating system and must be written to run on top of that particular operating system. As a user, you normally interact with the operating system through a set of commands. **And for the human "operating system," that's where goals, values, and purpose-setting comes in.** Our incredible brains process in similar ways to a computer system, with input, output, memory, and multitasking operations happening every second.

Bug Fixes and Upgrades

We are surrounded by technological advances, and every month something is being upgraded or improved. Anyone who has a smartphone, tablet, or laptop gets constant update announcements on their operating systems and apps. Along with the update, you usually get a bulleted list of what's being updated and improved. Our mind and body are also made up of systems, and we sometimes **need bug fixes and system updates and enhancements**. If you have a tooth cavity, it needs to be fixed. If you're easily winded from walking up the steps, you need to improve your cardiovascular system. If you watch television for 5 hours a day, you may need mental and physical exercise. Your spiritual health may be weak and in need of upgrades, or you may have "bugs" in your belief system.

One of the main purposes of this book and the 7 Gears program is to help you become the best version of your O.S. self so that you can connect your real capacity and potential to better results and outcomes. At your best, you can live a much more exciting life because of fulfilling your purpose and contributing beyond yourself.

What Operating Version Are You?

Just as computers can be upgraded, our thinking function can be upgraded! You create the blueprint-menu, either by design or default. You decide what it's going to be. Either **you** establish your life course or **someone else** will pull you into theirs; there's no in-between. What do we mean by versions of *you*? Humans, like all living creatures, run through operational lifecycle stages from conception to death. Author Martin Yate says in his book *Beat the Odds: Career Buoyancy Tactics for Today's Turbulent Job Market* that, "It's because the nature of work has changed that we have an economic climate where any company wanting to exist tomorrow must reinvent itself today."[17] Yate's book was published almost 20 years ago, but his words are even more relevant today. Just replace "company" with "[Your name], Inc." If we are to survive and flourish in our careers and personal development, it's important to constantly upgrade our knowledge, skills, and resourcefulness in order to stay in the game.

Stages of Life

We all pass through a series of different stages in life: from birth to toddler to early grade school, then to pre-teen and teen, young adult, adult, senior adult and senior. Like the rings in a tree, each stage's experiences remain in you, just at a different layer. Adult lifecycle author Vivian Rodgers McCoy tells us that "each stage is marked by a crisis, a turning point, a crucial point of both vulnerability and potential," and that "each period has specific tasks to be engaged in; when these are successfully engaged, we move on." McCoy adds, "It is the inner realm where crucial shifts of growth occur. How we feel about the marker events, especially off-timing or unanticipated life events, determines if we move on or stagnate."[18] Some of our "tree rings" are thinner than others due to lean years, drought years, or tough times. Opinions differ on just how many stages the human goes through, but it's agreed that there are between 4 and 9 stages. Greek philosopher Claudius Ptolemy believed there were seven stages of life, based in part on physical growth. From a modern perspective we could see these stages as operating system versions, always being upgraded or changed. The concept here is that we have a type of bio-computer system at work within us, with an extremely complex central nervous system. We are all running different versions in different life stages.

Change the Menu

Carte du Jour—What's on Your Life Menu?

Just as a restaurant has a Carte-du-jour, or a list of dishes that can be served that day, your "menu" tells us what's on your life menu. Gear 2 is all about planning and organization, an important factor in making your dream goals into tangible reality.

What's on the menu is what YOU put on the menu! You decide. **You are the chef** *and* **patron**. You create the menu (blueprint), either by design or default. You decide what it's going to be. It's worth repeating that either you establish your life course or someone else will pull you into theirs. Nobody really plans to fail, and yet it's been said that over 96% of folks just don't write their goals down. Those who make January resolutions statistically sustain about 2½ months into the year! But with the 7 Gears, your success rate percentage can change for the better!

Source Code

In the world of computers, a source code is a code that a programmer writes in high-level language to be read by humans but not computers. The Collins English Dictionary calls it "computing the original form of a computer program before it's converted into machine-readable code."

We too have our own **internal "source code"** by default and by design as DNA, talents, and unique propensities. I consider the source code to success to be what famous steel magnate Andrew Carnegie once told young journalist Napoleon Hill: "All success begins with Definiteness of Purpose." This purpose, "to be of enduring value, must be adopted and applied as a daily habit."[19] I would include that you must have a clear, multi-sensory image infused with intense desire.

Reprogramming Your Mind (System) for Upgraded Results

"Only a few find the way. Some don't recognize it when they do. Some...don't ever want to."

- The Cheshire Cat[20]

Getting from where you are to where you want to be calls for certain conditions to first be met. This second gear, **Operating System-Blueprint**, is the foundation in which all the successive conditions will be found for the remaining gears.

You and I have already been programmed through millions of experiences since birth. For instance, it's been calculated that more than 90 percent of your outside conditioning was negative, including being told "no" over 100,000 times by the age of 17. We've been programmed through a multitude of conditioning influences. Some of these include the place and environment of our upbringing and values instilled in us, along with the conditioning effects of rewards, punishments, friendships, family relationships, and millions of happy and unhappy experiences. Peer group associations, religious experiences, political beliefs, language, etiquette and protocols, and rules have all bombarded us with conditioning. All of these additive inputs have shaped your self-esteem, self-image, confidence, outlook on life, and your success rate in each of the eight goal areas we will be going over in this chapter. Since **none of us came into this world with an operator's manual,** it's all been trial and error, and we learn as we go.

A sharp, clear operating system is more than just having goals. In order to make the most of your internal operating system, you must set and define your Values, Purpose, and Identity *along with* your Goals. This is where many personal development plans end up missing some teeth (cogs) in their blueprint gear, because they simply throw down a few goals and leave it at that. However, the exciting thing about our conditioning is that it doesn't have to be permanent, like a read-only CD. Our operating systems can be upgraded for better results and life experiences.

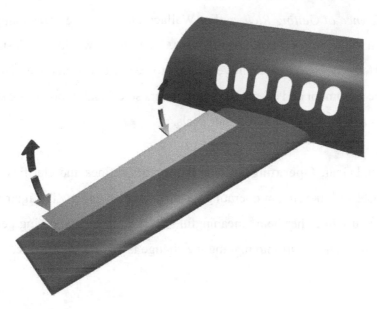

Your beliefs set the wing flaps that take you up or down

First, you must have a direction set in your guidance signal (this 2nd Gear).
Second, you need a course-correction mechanism (Values), which is your "GPS" to reference against your map, and then finally, you need sustained drive, or persistence fueled by a big reason (Purpose) **more compelling and empowering** than just a goal.

This second gear is foundational because it's the one that drives the next five gears all the way into the outcome, results, and Effect Gear. All outcomes and results are expressions and byproducts of the factors preceding them. Money is a byproduct of a value or service rendered.. Likewise, each of the 7 gears is additive. Like the tributaries of small creeks that flow into one river, the 7 gears compound their power and force, either in an upward direction or downward course.

In *The Science of Getting Rich*, author Wallace D. Wattle declares that you must do certain things in a **certain specific way**.[21] To obtain wealth, for instance, you must perform deliberate, definitive actions to reach that objective. That's what makes the alignment and sequence of the 7 gears so critical in obtaining successful outcomes and fulfilling more of your goals.

The Second Gear, **Operating System-Blueprint**, defines and clarifies your map (or template, or blueprint, or operating system). One of author Zig Ziglar's mantras was that you will either be a "meaningful specific" or a "wandering generality." Investing time and effort into making the change is *always* your choice.

Destiny-Shaping Tools

Self-Assessment

"If you don't know where you are, it won't matter where you're going."

- Bob Proctor[22]

An important factor in reaching your destination requires that you get a fix on where you are right now. Before we go any further, know this: **everyone has a bit**

of genius inside them. Everyone. That means you! Let's awaken that genius through the 7 Gears, starting with this one.

Why do we go in for a physical or a dental checkup? Because we want a perfectly functioning, healthy body. We want to measure the condition of our bodies, so we get the examination. It doesn't always mean there's a problem; it just catches any deviations from our fitness that might mean trouble in the future. It verifies that all your internal systems are indeed A-OK. **Any running machine or system requires diagnostics.** However, we are not just physical beings; we are made of spiritual, mental, and emotional aspects too. So why not do an internal operating system-blueprint checkup? We do it for our cars, why not for ourselves?

When you do the self-evaluation awareness exercises in this gear, you will be rewarded with improved command and control toward a more exciting destiny. In your self-evaluation, be sure to include what is running smoothly and working well for you, and what is not. Before setting off on a long journey in your car, you check engine fluids, fuel level, and tires for tread and air pressure. In addition to knowing what city they are leaving from, pilots run pre-flight checks and get under the plane they're about to fly by walking around and checking the condition of the tires, outer hull, etc.

One of the best destiny-shaping tools I've used in many business settings is what I call the **Where Am I Now? Map.** This method requires more space and time than this book can detail. Go to **www.the7gears.com** to get a copy of the customized guide. Coming up you will read many thought provoking questions meant to sharpen and clarify you into an empowered thinker. Consider every question put to you in this chapter and throughout the book as destiny shaping tools. Bring them all back to Gear 2 to strengthen and clarify your Operating

System. The rewards in doing so will pay you compound interest in value. Sharpen this Gear 2, and you sharpen all the others. In particular you will discover self-assessment type questions have a huge impact on the quality of Gear 6 Decision-Choice, the ultimate destiny shaping tool. Use every question to your advantage and profit.

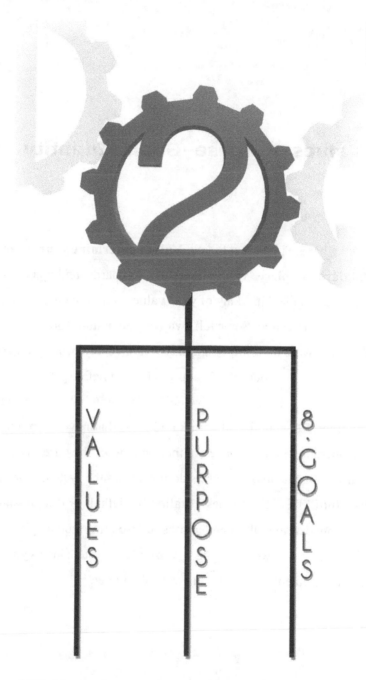

What makes up our operating system and our programs?

Values–Purpose–Goals–Identity

Values

Your values are what are important to you. **Values determine your priorities and put your standards in place**. Values are really standards, and when you violate your standards, you can feel it. Many of your values were not chosen by you; they were instilled in you as a child. Some fell away as you matured and grew, but some did not. Values that were once important may not have any bearing on you today. The importance of having your mom's approval on something, for example, may still be in place. Why? Because you value her opinion. There are many adult problems stemming from childhood values and rules that never were upgraded or changed. Our operating systems have another function: they are responsible for security, ensuring that unauthorized users do not access the system. For the human system, values fulfill this role. Values installed by default or design, stand guard and if violated, sound an alert through feelings of discomfort, unhappiness, anxiety or any negative emotion. A well-running **"gyro-value"** system keeps you level and able to withstand turbulent times and not get pushed over.

Strong values keep you balanced and level like a
Gyroscope Guidance System

Right now you have a value system in place. It *reveals itself* when you're faced with a decision or you need to prioritize a list of activities. There's a football game on Monday night at the same time as your son's Cub Scout pinewood derby. Which will you choose? *Values change* as we pass through different stages of career and home life. Twenty years ago, you may have had to decide between doing your piano practice or playing with your friends. Your value hierarchy today reveals what you consider important and how your values are closely tied in with your purpose, goals, and identity. Get these three "cogs" aligned and clear, and you will have a finely tuned system that, when aligned with the other gears, will make you unstoppable in manifesting the results and conditions you're after.

When clarifying your values, there are two good starting points that you can build from. First, **what do you believe in?** And honestly, what are you really willing to stand up for? Your values are important because they serve you later on as guidelines when making decisions, Gear 6. Your decision-making process will be quicker and smoother and will instantly be tested against your value system. Likewise, a strong, clear value set will work in instant tandem with Gear 5, your Feeling-Emotion Gear. When you're at a decision point, you get a "test report" that comes in the form of a feeling. When we say, "It just feels right," or, "Something's not right here!" that's your value system talking to you. Another benefit from a clear value system is that your decision-making faculty will be quick and decisive. Decisive actions are one of the key characteristics of leaders. No one bats 1000 on every choice; sometimes it comes down to a wild guess, but the probability of making wiser decisions will be much improved once you have your *value guidance system* in place.

Some of our values aren't so easy to spell out, and going through this process may call for a little extra effort. But you will be rewarded by having this part of your operating system in place. Here is a way for you to get your core values in place. Look over this list of popular values. If any of these resonate with you, add them to your existing value list. Pick your top seven and prioritize them.

Achievement	**Fulfillment**	**Love**
Balance	**Fun**	**Loyalty**
Character	**Generosity**	**Philanthropy**
Compassion	**Growth**	**Respect**
Competition	**Happiness**	**Security, job**
Easy Work	**Hard Work**	**Security, financial**
Fairness	**Health**	**Spontaneity**
Family	**Honesty**	**Stability**
Freedom	**Integrity**	**Tolerance**
Friendship	**Intelligence**	**Tradition**

If you're unhappy about a situation today, it probably traces back to a mismatch with your value system. Likewise, if you are generally happy, that traces to an alignment of your values. Many of life's difficulties can be traced back to a mismatch of our values with what we are doing at home or work or in a social situation. It comes as no surprise that most people are happy at work when they are delivering something of value **and** when their work is valued and appreciated.

As you will soon see, **your values are interlocked with your goals,** and when you change, your values alter accordingly. Follow these three construction steps:

- Values **assembled**
- Values **prioritized**
- Values **verified** to align with your goals, purpose, and identity

Your value system will adjust as you pass through different life stages and experiences.

By following these key pointers, you will shave off a lot of grief and frustration whenever you're faced with important decisions, which in turn will focus your actions toward getting what you want. Investing the time in this is honoring the Creator who gave us the gift of free will. And like in the parable of the talents (Matthew 25: 14–30), you're not hiding them but rather investing in yourself so that you can *be* the best, *do* your best, and *have* the best, with a life that's much more rewarding and on purpose.

Rules

Learned in childhood from our parents and teachers, rules are where we first form the **"BOX"** that we remain in when we "think inside the box" and "color inside the lines." In the same way, some of our self-imposed rules become a leash on our growth and life expansion. Our rules are tied to both our belief system and our value system. "If this, then that." Or, "I have to have _____ before I'm happy." On your life's bingo card, what do you need to have to be a winner? Or if you *don't* get that one thing, then you think you're a "loser"? In the first year of my marriage to Jeanette, our early arguments traced to a differing set of "rules" about how to carry on heated discussions. If you look at any relationship disagreement, whether it's personal or work-related, the source of diverging opinions traces back to an earlier adopted set of rules on how to deal with a problem or challenge.

Jeanette and I were able to trace our differences to rules of conduct learned in our formative family years. Her mom would slam cupboards in the kitchen when she was mad, while her dad simmered in silence. My mom and dad would shout, get loud, and explode at each other. With my dad, the argument was then over. My mom, on the other hand, might carry a grudge for weeks or months. And so Jeanette and I realized we needed to establish our own rules for future disagreements. And that has worked well, although engrained rules can still rear up, which goes to show you how powerful internal rules and values can be in our lives. Similar to hidden values, we can have dormant rules long since forgotten. Then one day you're faced with a challenging situation and - click! One of your hidden rules surfaces, and you act under its authority. As if under a post-hypnotic suggestion, you act accordingly and instantly without conscious thought. However, it IS possible for you to reprogram your values and rules.

It's important to **invest some time in getting clear on what your rules of operation are.** Ask your spouse or significant other what their rules are on disagreements, for example. It's surprising how many couples gloss over this as too trivial to even discuss. You may discover a hidden thing that irks your mate. That's good! You can then find common ground to set your own rules. We all have a set of conscious and unconscious preferences and beliefs on ways to approach problems and issues. There are going to be some rules, values and even beliefs you just may not agree on. But the quality of your relationship will be greatly enhanced if you can agree to respect the fact you may not share every rule or value priority list.

"The purpose of life is a life of purpose."

- Robert Byrne[23]

Purpose, Clearly Defined

It's been reported that over 95% of all people living today have no well-defined purpose in life! Lack of a well-defined purpose is one of the major causes of failure for most people. Following through and committing to apply the elements in this Gear alone will take you up and into the top 3%!

More often than not, your best clue when thinking about your purpose is to reflect back on what you've been good at, something others struggle with but you don't. Nothing is too small or insignificant when reflecting on any talent or ability. For you, it just seems to come easily. This usually starts showing up when you're young and in grade school. It could be math. It could be music or art, or home decorating, or a special skill in negotiating or leading a group. Some people are a natural with kids, crafts, carpentry, computers, or electronics. It could be anything. Ask a close friend or relative what they think you're good at.

When upgrading your purpose, it should be compelling and worthy. It should generate excitement and be inspirational. Another clue that you're on the right track when forming a clearly defined purpose is that it just feels good, really good. You somehow feel connected, aligned, light, even excited. **It just *feels* right.** You will feel an *urgency* to connect your goals into your purpose, your reason. This keeps you caring enough to want to reach your goals. If you know what comes easily to you and what you feel a passion for, you have found the pieces of what your purpose in life is. Richard Brodie, creator of Microsoft Word and author of *Getting Past OK: A Straightforward Guide to Having a Fantastic Life,* submits his perspective on the importance of having a clearly defined purpose and how it affects your ultimate direction. Brodie points out, "When you have a purpose, you *cause* things to happen in your life. When you don't, your life feels more like the *effect* of things happening to you."[24]

For those few who do take the time to really think about their purpose, they usually settle into one of three areas: 1) serving our **Creator,** 2) serving **others,** or 3) reaching their **full potential**. All of these are worthy purposes. May I suggest that instead of just picking one, you blend all three? If you think about it, all three of these are intertwined. No matter who you are or where you are, connecting with your true life purpose is a spiritual matter between you and God, which is why you will *feel it in your bones* and your very soul when you know your purpose.

You can have values and goals only and still make good progress, but odds are, you will end up beached on an island you're not happy with. When you have taken the time to clearly define your purpose, you will no longer be like a raft floating on water, buffeted by currents or the wind of circumstances. Having purpose puts a rudder, motor and a propeller on that raft.

When Purpose and Decision (Gear 6) are combined and aligned, your true compass is formed. Your true North is *your magnetic pull,* and your direction decisions puts on the needle. One more benefit is that having your purpose in place and in alignment with the upcoming gears will build a resistance to the doubts and fears that inevitably come at you in your success journey.

The Most Important Skill

One of the core themes running through these concepts is **communication**, communication *within ourselves* as internal dialogue, and *external* communication with family or business associates. Effective communication is critical and a defining factor in success or failure. Think of it as lubricating the gears to run more smoothly.

Is there some secret to how to communicate more effectively? The exciting answer is, **yes!** One of my favorite broadcast legends is Ty Boyd. He has one of the most dynamic speaking voices I've ever heard. The secret to communicating more effectively, Boyd says, is to **fire your purpose with passion!** He says to think about anyone who has ever moved you to action, like a teacher, coach, parent, business leader, or speaker.[25] At times you can even motivate yourself! You can be in a state where YOU influence yourself to make a change, or maybe an epiphany or flash revelation just comes to you.

This is why a flat affirmation without any emotion *has no real change power* in it. The more emotion you can inject into your values and goal-setting sessions, the more strength and perseverance you will have when you encounter the inevitable barriers, gaps, and diversions that will stand between you and your goal realization. As mentioned earlier, the reason for this is that intense emotions open a pathway into the subconscious, where our habit patterns are formed. Use your emotions to guide you on whether your values, purpose, and goals *strike fire in your soul*. If they do, you know you're on track. If they do not, then go back and make changes until you can feel these three elements in your bones! Have you ever gone clothes shopping and didn't know exactly what you wanted, but then saw something and knew it was right the instant you saw it? And remember the scene in *Christmas Vacation* when Clark Griswold suddenly sees *the* tree he wants for his living room? You will know it in your gut when you hit on the right purpose for you. There will be more on this in the chapter that covers the 5th Gear, Emotion-Feeling.

Purpose infused with your passion creates exciting results and outcomes. For example, Tom Brady, Donald Trump, Tom Cruise, Peyton Manning, Billy Graham, Tony Robbins, Richard Branson, Suze Orman, Joyce Meyer, Howard Schultz, Angelina Jolie, Oprah Winfrey, and Clint Eastwood have all worked with passion-infused purpose! These few models are only a small part of the total picture. The fact is, there are many more people who are not rich and famous but who are just as passionate about their hobbies, work or areas of interest. Most likely, someone you know right now fits this description, someone at your work or place of worship, a medical expert, the instructor in a class you're taking; it could be anybody, anywhere. These are local, everyday folks who have that spark, that extra something. If you study people who are successful in their field, and yours, you can find clues to model or learn from, just as they did. Every champion in every field has mentors and coaches. No one is a solo act. Treat this book as one of your personal coaches.

Don't "Follow Your Passion"

You shouldn't have to *follow* your passion, as the popular mantra goes. If all of the power factors found in this gear are applied and internalized, you won't be distanced by your passion. It won't be somewhere *out there* like a holiday tour guide ahead of you to be sought after and then followed. Your true passion is already within you waiting to be acknowledged, activated and steered.

Yes, you should seek the type of work you love, but I'm not suggesting leaving your day job tomorrow. If your present job isn't fulfilling or doesn't seem to have the future you're looking for, make changes wisely. Start where you are with what you have control over. For now, look for something you *can* be passionate about, such as a hobby, while still finding parts of your job you *can* be on fire about. If you really think about it, every job is temporary. Every job, no matter what it is, has something that you can learn from and use in your next adventure. Even if you're presently working in unhappy conditions, you can use the experience to a future advantage. Bad examples, while costly and uncomfortable, add to your career wisdom and knowledge base. Expect them as stepping stones to your upward career path. You can use the temporary occurrence to supply you with wisdom and strength, which are leadership characteristics that you can make use of later on, if and when you move into a higher leadership position. When you take this approach, you can still be moving in the direction you desire and have something to inspire you along the way. If you include this advice and apply what you have learned in this chapter, then you will accelerate your progress in the direction *you* want to go.

A big enough WHY or **reason,** can be like the bellows that fan the coals of desire and passion. Find reasons; stack them up! We will go more into the magical power of reasons as a rocket booster in the chapter on State of Mind. All champions and so called stars can serve as models of possibility. Every one of the people mentioned above first had models, mentors and life examples they looked up to, just as you can right now! What would cause you to leap out of bed every morning? And don't say "a million dollars," because that's a *means* value, not an end. Valued **means** is a *way* to get something, but valued **ends** delivers the emotional *feeling* that comes from obtaining your objective. For instance, you want the red California Ferrari (means) for the thrill and exciting feelings (ends) it would generate. Another proof that your purpose is right on is that it will be compelling enough to get you highly motivated.

You will see the multiplying effect of the upcoming Faith-Belief, Perspective-Viewpoint, and Emotion-Feeling Gears and how they combine to create an unstoppable power state. If all three of these gears are turned up, look out! **Passion, purpose, and confidence** will come through automatically. You won't have to work at it (another clue that you're spot on, in the groove). All this, put together, will create a passion in your communication within yourself and outwardly in your work. *Purpose infused with fire of enthusiasm is the best kind of purpose.*

A purpose is not the same as a goal. Your purpose is a lifelong compass and guide, whereas goals have a beginning and an end. You can have purpose and values but still let them just sit there powerless, like a battery that's not hooked up to anything. It will just sit there until it is connected into a circuit of something that pushes it into motion.

Think through these guide points to sharpen up your purpose. This should be fun!

- When are you, or were you, happiest?
- Think of a time when you were involved in something that was **satisfying.** It was so **fun and exciting** that you would jump out of bed in the morning to get back at it. Because the work or project was so gratifying, it wasn't work; it was fun! Without realizing it, you were working "on purpose."
- What comes naturally to you? What do others struggle with that you don't? What have you done in the past that caused you to lose all sense of time?
- **If money were no object,** what is the FIRST thing you would do?
- **If money were no object,** what is the SECOND thing you would do? (This can be more revealing than the first thing as to your true values.)
- What accomplishments are you **most proud of**? Why?
- What do people ask your advice or help on? How could you use your talents or abilities to benefit a group or cause?
- Who do you greatly respect, and why?
- If you **could change one thing** at your work place, what would that be and why? Then what would to do with that change?
- **If your house were on fire**, in order of priority what four things would you race back to get (if all living beings were already safe)?
- What are your top five values in order of importance?

Now you must take the private time to really soul search and write these down! Share your notes with no one! This is actually between you and your co-pilot

Creator. This should never be a struggle if you let your heart and soul guide you. Use Gear 1, Attention-Awareness, and especially your 6th sense, which is the conduit and tapping point of all opportunity and infinite possibilities. I believe it is also one of God's pathways of that "still, small voice" that delivers answers you prayerfully seek. The 7 Gears operate bi-directionally. Sometimes those answers appear from the other direction and through any one of the other gears. People and circumstances will come to you that are exactly what you're looking for or needing. Your friends and acquaintances may call it serendipity, but you will know otherwise because of what you have learned and applied within these chapters. If you feel fear about acting on any of these ideas, use the energy of that feeling to take action anyway, and you will be surprised at how the fear was just fog. So walk into it, get on the other side, and feel thankful for your chance to contribute value to the world and for the ecstatic feeling that comes with living your life on purpose—your purpose.

You—yes, YOU—absolutely, positively have some unique, special skill or talent that the world needs and wants! Our Creator has intentionally placed more than one seed-purpose within you, and they are as exclusive as your fingerprints. Some seed-purposes run the length of life, while others may reveal themselves and sprout years later. Sadly, millions of people never seek or recognize their special gift of purpose and spend out their precious gift of life as drifting vagabonds. But, hey! You're reading this book right now; **you** have the wonderful, exciting opportunity not to let that happen. You hold in your hands the "password" to get you into the rich, rewarding life you are meant to have!

With no purpose, you will always be the cork bobbing on the water, the "victim" we mentioned earlier. So don't pass this off as something you'll get to someday.

Someday is NOW! With your updated and clearly defined purpose, you will be empowered with determination and resolution and in control of your destiny.

A well-defined purpose will:
- ✓ serve others;
- ✓ be a part of something bigger than your goals;
- ✓ reveal itself to you when you're sincerely ready, and will be validated by *feeling right.*

An investment in getting clear and definite on your purpose adds another cog in your **Operating System-Blueprint Gear** and will reward you later by making Gears 6 and 7 run more smoothly.

Goals: The Great Human Enigma

Everyone has heard of setting goals. If it's not so hard, then why doesn't everybody do it? Here are some of the top reasons:

1. They <u>don't understand the true value</u> and importance of goal setting.
2. They <u>don't know the right way</u> to set them.
3. If they do set goals, it's a <u>halfhearted</u> effort because of being jaded from "too many" past failures. Remember the earlier statistic about New Years' resolutions that last about six weeks?
4. We all fail to achieve some of our goals, and <u>who wants to return</u> to that feeling again?

In spite of the fad "manifestation" tools and techniques that are always popping up, there is still nothing to replace the effectiveness of setting worthwhile goals. *Everything* you do will come under at least one of these eight goal areas:

The Eight Primary Goal Areas
Everything to the Eight!

Goal area #1   FINANCIAL

Goal area #2   EDUCATIONAL/Knowledge/Skill/Ability

Goal area #3   RELATIONAL—Personal/Business

Goal area #4   CAREER/Profession

Goal area #5   FAMILY/Home/Recreational

Goal area #6   MENTAL/SPIRITUAL

Goal area #7   PHYSICAL/Body/Health/Vitality

Goal area #8   SERVICE—Giving back to community/Charity

Gear 2, Operating System-Blueprint, sets the quality and strength of how all other gears will function. Figure out where you are right now in each of the Eight Primary Goal areas as a benchmark. NOW you can move on to the goal-setting process! It's important to **recharge your goal vision and purpose every day**, each time emotionally experiencing the rewards waiting for you at the finish line.

"My success in business has largely been the result of my ability to focus on long-term goals and ignore short-term distractions. Taking a long-term view doesn't require brilliance but it does require dedication."

- Bill Gates[26]

I believe author and speaker Brian Tracy has written the most definitive book on the subject, *Goals! How to Get Everything You Want—Faster Than You Ever Thought Possible.* Tracy says that if he had only five minutes to express the one most successful idea, it would be, "Write down your goals, make plans to achieve them, and work on your plans every single day."[27] The tried-and-true **S.M.A.R.T.** template works well here. If you've never heard of it, follow this template when writing out your eight goal areas:

Specific – Make each goal specific and exact.

Measurable – In dollars, volume, time, experiences

Action Plans – Describe your action plan to make it happen.

Realistic – Set some goals with an **80/20, 60/40**, and **50/50** probability. They should be exciting—not too far out, not to easy.

Timed – Set a date and time deadline. Have long-term 10-year lifestyle goals, as well as 5-year, 3-year, 1-year ½-year, and monthly time frames.

Let's Get SMART-ER

There is something you can do to make your goal-setting process even **"SMART*ER*."** *Smarter* goal setting includes **E.**—*experience:* replay over and over the sensory-rich feelings and excitement of your goal realized, in the present moment, as if it were happening right now; and **R.**—*repeat*: repeat your goal "mental movie" at least three times a day, preferably before going to bed and again upon arising. If necessity is the mother of invention, **repetition is the father of all**

progress. And that's what we're after: progress. Some say we should set all goals at a **50/50** chance of making it. I believe that's good for some goals, but you need to have some early successes that prove to your mind that the system works. And for that reason, set some goals with an **80%** chance of completing, some at **60%,** and some at **50%.** This combination will give you positive feedback and momentum.

What's Your GPA?

No, it's not your grade point average; it's *the big three* in the goal-setting process. **GPA** is an easy way to keep your focus on the key ingredients: **Goals, Plans** and **Actions.** You need all three to make goal achievement work. Taking *consistent forward-moving action,* though, is where most people fall away.

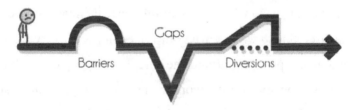

Why? Because they encounter one or more of these three challenges: barriers, gaps, and diversions. Folks either have enough drive and desire to get over and through them, or they get waylaid. But none of these barriers, gaps, and diversions you encounter have to be show-stoppers. That is, IF you are prepared and armed with a winning strategy and sufficient drive and persistence get past all of them. You hold in your hands the tools, techniques, and information to make that happen!

Author and speaker Bob Proctor has added something to effective goal setting, and that is to include the gratitude preamble *"I'm so happy and grateful now that...,"* and then add your **SMART** present-tense, positive, short goal to it.[28] You must also have strong feeling and emotion with each goal. Remember, it's *emotion* and *repetition* that get us past the subconscious "goalie" and that gets a goal seed planted with a real chance of germinating into reality. There are two more proven essentials in making the most of effective goal setting. One is to end your goal statement using *"-ing"* ("I am so happy and grateful now that I am complet*ing* my degree by December 15th."). Last, but not least, is to be *in* your goal picture, not an observer. You must feel the experience with all the emotion and thrill of that day as if it's happening now.

The preceding ideas are a distillation of the masters on the subject. In the interest of cutting out the fluff and gimmicks, follow and apply these basic rules. Make sure your goals are challenging and exciting and that they align with your core values and purpose. One final mandate is that you must write every goal down **on paper** and have them at hand where you can reference them at least weekly. If you can muster the discipline to write down your top eight goals every week, they will be strongly engrained, putting you into the rare 3% of people who know how to make their goal-setting experience work. The stronger you can visualize and experience each goal with all your senses, the better. And if you believe you're not a vivid visualizer, then define your goal if you were describing it to someone right in front of you. By the way, what color is your refrigerator? Aha, you most likely just visualized it!

Goals Are Not All about Taking and Getting

I have two hints about how to set your goals in a way that works. First, include in your mental/spiritual goals a commitment to build your character strength to a level that makes you unstoppable in going after the results and outcomes you're after. If you apply what you learn in this book, you will understand that Goal Area #8 (Service) is more than just providing some of your time or money. Up ahead in the

128

Gear 3 chapter, you will see a "prime the pump" graphic that depicts the foundational reciprocity principle that *you must give before you can get*. This not only applies to goal area 8, Service, but is also a key element in successful negotiations, whether business or personal. You must include this in your goal-defining sessions. What do you plan to give *before* you get? According to your giving be it unto you. Making some form of genuine, heartfelt contribution has been shown to have an effect on your long-term health and longevity. Our Creator designed us to give back and contribute in some unique way.

Most People Are Starving Right Now

Goal area #8 (Service) includes giving sincere praise and appreciation when and where they are due. Gaining attention is the pathway to recognition. Children instinctively know this and will risk the chance it may not work. When appreciation and praise are missing in any relationship, self-esteem malnutrition sets in like a vitamin/mineral deficiency. Think back—how did you feel when your parent, brother, sister, or trusted role model gave you praise or accolade? How about when you received no appreciation for something you put your heart and soul into? Children crave attention from their parents and are masters at getting it, whether it's through favorable or unfavorable ways and means. As adults, that hunger still resides within us. I submit that it's the favorable attention we may receive on our birthday or at work that we enjoy more than the gift or award itself. Giving praise and appreciation should be a lifelong habit. Valued appreciation must be sincere, spontaneous, and never contrived. One honest expression of heartfelt praise has the power to change lives, both yours and theirs! Start this habit today before the sun sets! Children, co-workers, subordinates, staff, and spouses all need the nourishment of praise and appreciation. You will reap a fabulous side effect of more enjoyable and rewarding relationships. Even if *you're* "starving" right now, go first and light the candle of warm attention and appreciation to those around you. If you're serious about setting goals that are most rewarding, then invest the time to follow through on this part of Service goals that gives back to your community. Some goal areas are "**go-getter**" goals, and some are "**go-giver**" goals. *We need both* if we are to experience a rich, fulfilling life with meaning and significance.

Goal Setting on Steroids: "The Big Six"

When you write out your goals, test them against the "Big Six" questions of **Who, What, When, Where, Why and How**. Do not treat this step lightly! Applying this deceivingly simple exercise will be worth it because the answers you get will help strengthen and clarify all three legs of Value, Purpose, and Goals in a way that will surprise you! If you're serious about making big changes and improvements in the quality of your life, then you will do this simple exercise today. More importantly, you'll make it a weekly habit to fine tune your eight goal areas. One more tip on making the most of using question power: **Ask more *How* questions than *If* questions.** As author M.R. Kopmeyer says, "Never ask 'IF' anything can be improved; always ask 'HOW' you can improve it."[29] In the world of real estate, it's about *location, location, location*. For goal setting that works, it's about *clarity, clarity, clarity*.

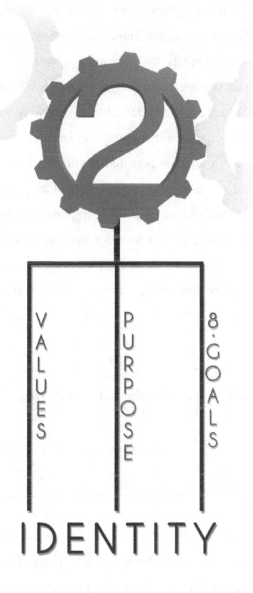

The Three Legs Are Held Together by Your IDENTITY

These three legs—values, purpose, and goals—are central to your **personal identity.** A person's identity is formed from a combination of ties ranging from career, religion, role models, family and social relationships, or abilities you discovered you had growing up. Additionally, a positive sense of self comes from the collection of achievements that were important to you. Getting a clear understanding of who you are at this stage in your life is an important factor in making the level of change you're after. Here's the tricky wicket: ironically, it's important to *not* fasten your identity to your *outcomes*. This is where many people get hurt when they don't separate personal identity from an undesirable result or condition. If you fall short, exercise your faith and long-term viewpoint to keep your perspective. If you exceed your expectations and goals, be humble and thankful. In either outcome, always look for the lesson so you can approach the next challenge wiser and stronger. You paid for the lesson, so grab the lesson and go. If you remain loyal to upstanding Values, Purpose and Identity, your strength of character will shield you from those who would try to manipulate you or take advantage of you.

> *"Be certain that you do not die without having done something wonderful for humanity."*
>
> - Dr. Maya Angelou, *Letter to My Daughter*

"Fools Goals"

In Colorado, miners in the 1800s were caught up in the Pike's Peak gold rush. Most of those panning for gold would bring up iron pyrite known as "fool's gold" because it shone like gold but actually had no value. It's ironic that Central City, Colorado was once known as "the richest square mile on earth." One hundred and fifty years later, Central City draws a new generation of "fools," as it's the biggest gambling and casino area in the state.

You've figured out by now that this book isn't about how to win in Vegas. I acknowledge, though, that there are certain games like Blackjack where you can influence a winning hand based on your knowledge of statistics. So to some extent, we are talking about gaining enough knowledge and skill for increasing the odds of a better hand. Success means different things for different people. It's not for me to judge other people's wants and desires. Just be careful that your values and goals based on material things such as huge homes, fast cars and jewelry aren't your first priority. A recent research project conducted on terminally ill people who only had a short time left on earth showed that all had common answers about what they most regretted in life. Most said they wished they had invested more time in friends and family relationships.

There is a long-term benefit from going through the exercises in this chapter. When you take the time and effort to sincerely get clear on your true values and priorities, you will eliminate much grief and frustration later on. You will most likely not get caught up in the empty glitter of goals and dreams that would otherwise leave you jaded, unhappy, and disillusioned. You will know your goals are on target when they fire up your enthusiasm. Having goals in all eight areas should help to ensure that you're balanced in material and non-material desires. When you sit down and really think through your identity and value statements, understand the futility of tying your full identity and self-worth to your accomplishments and failures.

Just know that in the *natural process* of goal reaching, the satisfaction and warm glow of accomplishing your goals will flash and then fade like a Fourth-of-July sparkler. And that's not a bad thing; the great feeling is good, and you've earned it. It's part of the reward. But you must realize that it's all part of the great *cycle of events*. When you keep this high-level perspective and your eight goal areas are set and feel right, then you will be able to bridge this challenge. Goals should not be carved in stone; they should be *dynamic and upgradeable,* because life is in motion, and unforeseen changes can alter your life course. Priorities are always under review, and they change either by intent or default. Surprising opportunities or changes in conditions can also affect your goals. So don't be too rigid in the goal-setting process. **You should be resolute in your objective, but flexible and agile in what actual path gets you there.**

The Unicycle and the 4-Wheel Drive

Having only one of these four elements of Gear 2 is like riding a unicycle: you can move forward, but it will be slower and more difficult. Having two of these in place is like a bicycle; you can move faster along, but whenever you get stalled or the hill is too steep you will fall over. With three wheels in place, you can at least balance when you stall, but you could still get tipped over. But having all four— **Values, Purpose, Goals, and clear Identity**—is like having a four-wheel drive vehicle that can stand up to the inevitable hills, curves, and high winds.

Persistence

One final important piece to serious, effective goal setting is *persistence.* Doing everything in this chapter will put you ahead of the less-persistent 95 percent. Yet there is still one more part to the goal-setting formula, and that's having a **high enough level of persistence** to keep going, no matter what. Every champion is relentless in the pursuit of his or her goals and objectives. And I'm referring to more than just superstar athletes and celebrities; I'm talking about cancer survivors, disabled military veterans, single moms and dads, substance abuse victims, and anyone with any kind of affliction or physical, mental or emotional challenge. **Perseverance is the common denominator** required to ensure you reach your goals. Persistence is a common thread among champions, and there will be more on this subject in subsequent chapters.

Tripping Point

Everyone at one time or another gets tripped up in moving toward a goal, and it's usually over something small, so when it happens, try to **fall forward**, not back. The "tripping" we're talking about here is an internal mental thing, not physical. This approach to so-called setbacks is another one of those little things that can prove to make a huge difference later on. An old Japanese proverb says, "When you fall down, do not get up empty handed." Every successful person passes through many "failings," which are really nothing more than neutral outcomes and results until we attach an emotional label to them! One of the key causes to setting low-par goals is the fear of not making it! However, by investing in each of these 7 gears, this problem falls away, because you will have the horsepower to break through barriers, leap over gaps, and push past most diversions that are waiting to stop your goal-getting progress.

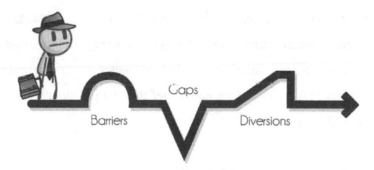

Challenging experiences build strength of character, which in turn prepares you for the bigger, better rewards.

Do Affirmations Really Work?

Yes, and no. There's been a lot of discussion floating around personal development circles about the effect or non-effect of affirmations. Why does it seem to work for some but not others?

Using affirmations that work is like flying a kite. Conditions, materials, and design must all be right before you can get a kite up in the air. The wind must be steady and not too rough, and the string must be thin, light, and strong. The kite's design and materials must be well constructed. You have to be facing the right way in the wind. And so it is with affirmations; there are right ways and wrong ways of using them.

Getting affirmations to "fly" follows some of the rules we learned in forming goals, values, and purpose statements. Napoleon Hill gave us one clue about effective affirmations back in 1937 when he said, "A mind dominated by positive emotions becomes a favorable abode for the state of mind known as faith. A mind so dominated may, at will, give the subconscious mind instructions, which it will accept and act upon immediately."[30] Emotionally charged visualization is the language the subconscious tunes into and acts on. **Sensory-rich** pictures with you *in* them that are repeated daily have a better chance of taking hold of your programming. By "taking hold," I mean **belief** that is in resonance with both the conscious and subconscious.

How It's Framed and How It's Aimed

The problem, however, with most affirmations is that most are directed at the 10% conscious mind instead of at the subconscious level. Even positive affirmations are no match for a deep-seated negative belief entrenched at the subconscious level.

This is why many basic popular affirmations create internal resistance, frustration and conflict.

If, for example, you were to firmly declare to yourself, "I am a genius," you would hear a voice inside you screaming back, "Not true!" The internal battle gets underway, with the deep-seated belief of "I'm not that smart" winning out. And that's the problem; the subconscious mind does not accept it as a belief yet because it's too weak to cause any real change. Like the children's game of "king of the hill," the dominant belief stays on top.

Change Your Approach and...
Change Your Results

An interesting study of experiments conducted on two different approaches to motivating self-talk was made public in 2010 by Senay, Albarracín, and Noguchi. The two approaches were defined as A) making an affirmation structured as a *declaration*, and B) self-talk sentences framed as a type of *interrogation* Interrogation- style affirmations structured as a question showed conclusive evidence that telling ourselves is much weaker than posing a question to ourselves.[31] If you find yourself declaring, "I can never seem to earn enough income to cover my bills," that's an affirmation that chokes off thinking about creative options. That kind of declaration creates negative tension. Interestingly, a more positive affirmation such as, "I always have more than enough income to handle any bill," may sound good but can still create internal resistance if it isn't really, really believed at the deepest level.

Referring back to the example above, what if, instead of declaring, "I am a genius," you pose the thought as a question such as, "Have I ever done anything that was

137

brilliant or above average?" And then, "Will I come up with another great idea?" This leads to, "If I did it before, how can I do it again?" This opens your thoughts to coming up with something you *did* do well that others might have called "genius." You may realize, "Well, yeah! There was that one time I figured out how to cut costs in shipments that has saved the company thousands of dollars annually! And I remember that time when I..." In this approach, the difference is in **altering "I will "declarations into "Will I, have I?" interrogations.** Another proven sandwich affirmation method is to state one key action you declare you will do today after your question. This proves and validates to your belief-feeling guard that it's ok to let the idea pass. It assures your subconscious that this is really happening! For example: "I am getting better at organizing my day. What one thing will I do to improve my organization skills? I will respond only to important emails from 9–10 a.m., then move on to the next priority." There's something about asking a question that disarms the subconscious defense mechanism from its deep-rooted beliefs, positive or negative. And that gets you closer to the all-important alignment of your two minds. You can leverage the method further by adding, "Can I?" or "What if..?" or "If Jane did it, can I?" Using "Is there a way?" as a starter question will then enlist the friendly assistance of your supercomputing subconscious, which in turn will start churning out ideas and options! This is one of those little gears that can turn bigger gears. Now instead of ramrodding the fortress gate of the subconscious through endless repetitions of affirmative declarations, you now have its cooperation and support!

Now Use Your Wording

In spite of these new findings, there still are those who have had positive affirmations work for them, but most likely because they unwittingly had congruency between their conscious and subconscious. Affirmations are personal, like clothing, food, or jewelry preferences, and they need to resonate with *you.*

138

They need to **feel just right**—something **only** *you* will know is right when you "try one on." Modeling other peoples' exact affirmations may not fit you and therefore won't work. However, the more you can practice creating a sensory-rich goal movie during your affirmation session, the faster the subconscious will convert it to an order.

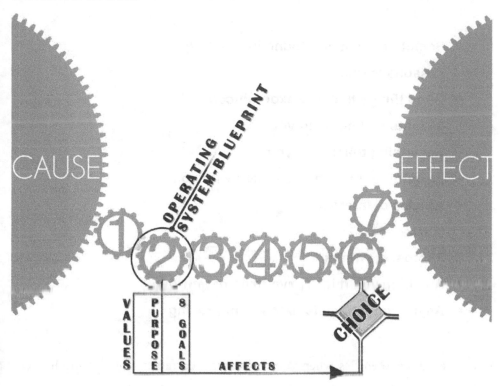

The clarity of your Values, Purpose, and Goals
affects the quality of your decisions

The Value of Keeping an Active Journal

In addition to the power of goal setting, there is an empowering habit called journaling: writing down insightful comments and perspectives for the day, week or recent event you've experienced. Today there are a number of ways to record your life lessons, progress and valuable experiences. Smart phones, tablets, and computers can all be easy-access methods to make journal entries. I've found that there's something powerful in the experience of actually writing it down on paper. The whole process should be enjoyable and fulfilling. **Make note of the following:**

- **Something that you found interesting**
- **Lessons learned**
- **Good things that you experienced**
- **Insights that come to you**
- **Something that upset you**
- **Inspiring quotes that resonate with you**
- **Articles of interest**
- **Milestones**
- **Photos, drawings**
- **Anything you might have fixed or improved**
- **Anything that needs fixing or improving**

It's better to make entries when you feel compelled rather than forcing it every day. It needs to flow effortlessly. This whole process will sharpen your thinking, cause you to be conditioned to new opportunities, and give you a look back at how you have grown or gotten through an experience that, in retrospect, wasn't that big after all. One last thing about your journaling habit: **don't share it with anyone.** Like your purpose, it's too sacred and personal to be exposed to any ridicule or outside comment. This is to be between you and the experience. However, later on, your journals can be of value to your kids as life-lesson hand-me-downs, because they will most likely contain bits of wisdom that your family can benefit from.

When we evaluate our outcomes and the results of our efforts, a belief in what's next is formed. We therefore MUST build on every success, even if it's partial, even if it's small, because successes shape our belief system.

Worth Remembering

- A purpose is more compelling than a goal, but you still need both.

- Stress and challenges will test the strength of your Values, Beliefs, and Purpose and temper your Identity and Character.

- Those with a weak Gear 2 usually live more reactively than proactively.

- Your clearly defined goals and values will favorably affect all other gears, especially your Decision-making gear.

- When making choices and decisions (Gear 6), your Values, Purpose, and Goals will guide you with instant feedback by your feelings: "It just feels right," or, "It just feels wrong."

- There is no gray area between honesty and dishonesty.

- Having clarified your goals and values, you will more quickly make course corrections if you get off track. You will also avoid more disasters and lost time.

- Having completed this gear, you just jumped ahead of 95% of the population!

- A well-defined Purpose backed with Values and Goals sharpens your Identity and puts cause and meaning into your life. A well-defined Purpose increases the value of your *life game chips.*

- Goals start and end. Your purpose is your ongoing lifelong North Star guide.

- Realize that *every* question put to you in this book are destiny shaping tools.

- Summary: When your <u>Operating-System-Blueprint</u> changes, your experiences and conditions change!

<u>Worth Doing</u>

- Draw out the Gear 2 graphic showing values, purpose, goals, and identity, then fill it in. The tIme you invest in this will generate compound interest for you later on.

- Make reaching your goals and staying on purpose a more valuable source of pleasure than instant gratification!

- If you would only commit to one thing, commit to improvement and progress—<u>Sustained Unwavering Progress</u> through your <u>Daily Action Habits: SUP-DAH!</u>

- Divide and conquer a goal that might be too daunting at first. Change the probability ratio from 50/50 to 80/20.

- Everyone gets tripped up on the way to a goal, and it's usually in the little things, so always <u>fall forward</u>. D*on't get up empty handed; take your new bit of wisdom with you.*

- If working on your major goals feels painful and too costly, something's wrong. Go back and refine your Purpose, Values and Identity statements until they all feel right and congruent, or look into the divide and conquer technique mentioned above.

- Use every series of questions as destiny shaping tools

- Make a lifetime commitment to build your strength of character if you want champion status.

- Assemble your Purpose to include work that goes beyond just yourself and involves helping others.

- Be on the lookout for positive role models. The best ones may not be rich and famous or far away. Find at least one for each goal area.

- Convert your values and purpose questions into a do-it action. Apply at least one of your purpose-shaping questions.

Your Operating System–Blueprint (Gear 2) drives...

Gear •3

FAITH-BELIEF

"… according to your faith be it unto you."

(Matt. 9:29)[32]

The Elixir of Miracles

For good reason, volumes have been written about the power of faith, hope, trust and belief. For centuries it's been the foundation to all religions and faiths. It is also the "sine qua non," **the essential ingredient**, to tapping unlimited potential and opportunity and converting them to reality. Groups like Alcoholics Anonymous acknowledge and trust that there is a higher power who can work with us and through us if we have enough faith. Legions of people, myself included, would line up to give you their testimony about how strong faith has changed or even saved their lives. Faith is not a material thing like natural gas or crude oil that is hidden away in limited supply. I believe our Creator purposely made the invisible **well of faith** to be *always* available and *always* ready to be drawn up. Faith and Belief is a combined ***thought-feeling-action*** blend that is unlimited in supply. The chapter on State of Mind will reveal more detail on how to make Faith and Belief work.

Faith-Belief: Static or Applied? You Decide

Obtaining Beliefs works like a valve that taps into the "keg" of any possibility, healing energy, support, or answers we might seek. The valve of belief can be set to a trickle or wide open to gush like a fire hydrant. It is always our hand on that valve, no one else's. A person's beliefs are a self-assembled collection of "truths" and perspectives, either empowering or disempowering.

The conduit of faith more often than not defies human logic. You can't calculate or predict when, where, or how the promise of applied faith will deliver. Maybe that's why exercising faith is not always easy. To get into an empowered state we need the blended thought-feeling-action, but **prayer and meditation** also give us the alignment we need to open the valve. This is what we were talking about with

Gear 1: Attention-Awareness and "The Man From U.N.C.L.E." analogy of opening "channel D." Only in this case, we're opening Channel B as the channel of *Belief!*

Please read this again! This concept is so deceptively simple and yet so powerful! I have been guilty so many times of glossing over this point because of being caught up in a disempowering state, or just simply losing sight and awareness of how powerful this key to the kingdom is!

You may ask, "Just how do I increase this gear of Faith and Belief enough to make a difference?" I will give you a heads-up: you must also apply the 7th Gear of Action. "Faith by itself, if it is not accompanied by action, is dead" (James 2:17).[33] **You can't approach Faith and Belief as an observer;** faith must be *internalized*. It doesn't work as something that's just "out there." You will see how Gear 6, Decision-Choice, is really the *first* required action that turns the valve on. You must **choose** faith over fear, choose faith over doubt, and choose faith over discouragement. **You don't observe faith; you absorb and internalize it to make it work in your life.** But first you must commit to faith by saying, "Yes, let's do this together! I *will* believe it's possible. Yes, I can do it, and yes, I have a greater power at my side as my co-pilot." So hang in there. We're just getting into the full process of the 7 Gears and how each plays a part in delivering the kinds of outcomes you seek.

Great Expectations

At this moment, right now, there is a level of motivating energy contained in your expectations. And we *all* have expectations in each of the eight goal areas mentioned in the previous chapter. There is an ongoing dynamic self-set **level of expectation** for everything you do, which can reside at an unconscious level. It

149

remains hidden until you're faced with a task, challenge, or goal, and then it reveals itself. You know it, because you can feel it. No matter what goal area, if your outlook is set low, your "try power" drops accordingly. There's a hidden psychological reason behind those who keep expectations low: you won't get disappointed that way. Sadly, that form of pessimism grows into a long-term downward spiral. Psychologist William James stated, "Belief creates the actual fact," a statement of profound importance to your future destiny![34]

I believe that you have some ideas that the world could benefit from, waiting inside you just like seeds waiting to be planted and grown. Walt Disney once sat on a park bench watching his daughters play at an unkempt, unsafe amusement park and got the *seed-idea* that there needed to a cleaner, nicer, better amusement park that that even parents could enjoy. The reality of Disneyland wouldn't exist today if Disney had let go of his faith to pursue his vision.

There is another benefit from the work you put in on **Gear 2** setting **Values, Purpose, and Goals**: the act alone of setting and clarifying your goals has a positive effect on your belief system. Setting your values, beliefs, and goals brings with it a new spark of hope, that first level of certainty that things are going to be better.

Belief Systems

All beliefs really are parts of a system. Beliefs don't just snap into place or click on for no reason or without cause. There is a system of **connecting factors** that lead to "in-your-bones" beliefs, both empowering and disempowering. Remember that we said the subconscious mind does not hear the word "no;" it takes and processes everything as a "yes." A conditioned belief message is either, "Yes, I can do this," or "Yes, I cannot do this." As Henry Ford said, "Whether you think you can, or you think you can't—you're right."

Our belief systems run on two levels:
1. What you *CAN* do—what you believe is possible with and through a higher power beyond yourself.
2. What *YOU* can do—what you believe you can do within yourself.

You need both **faith in yourself** and **faith in the higher power**, the Creator. Just as a commercial airliner requires a pilot and co-pilot, we all need a pilot-co-pilot partnership. There is one big difference; our copilot has infinite power and potential. Just knowing that should make you very excited! Miracles do happen, and when you believe in *yourself*, your co-pilot *Creator*, and the *goal vision* you're working toward, you have ignition; you have liftoff!

Your evaluation of something today is biased according to the lifetime accumulation of thousands of mini-beliefs from your past. To some extent, you attract what you expect. It's not what you always want, but it is always what you expect. If your beliefs are limiting and disempowering either consciously or unconsciously, they will most certainly affect all the succeeding gears in line all the way to the outcome. You must maintain the ongoing habit of keeping an *open mind,* because without it you choke off the air needed for inspiration, faith, and belief to stay alive and prove itself to you.

The Elements of Faith, Hope, and Trust

Evaluations—Opinions

There is really no such thing as *no* belief. We always believe something. You either believe in faith, hope, and trust, or you believe there is no such thing. Your belief system is either mostly positive or mostly negative. Even though most of us have been taught not to be judgmental or biased, we are. Our beliefs are always on, always working, always judging. Yes, judging.

Scale of Positive & Negative Beliefs

We are always evaluating our experiences, our decisions, and other people. This includes everyone you meet, everyone you know, or even know of. We evaluate friends, family, acquaintances, and celebrities. Aren't conversations about celebrities just dialogues full of evaluations? *"Did you see what she wore at the Oscars?" "That politician is an idiot!"; "Isn't Johnny Depp the living end?"* And we are always evaluating ourselves: our abilities, our hair, our clothing, how we handled a recent situation. ***Let's get real! The truth is that we're all judging, evaluating, and biasing. Always!***

We all have an internal scale that is always active when we are awake. It's weighing the plus side against the minus side, forming opinions and beliefs. This mental-emotional scale evaluates in the flash of a second and then stores that micro-decision in your computer mind database. That decision will be used to influence your next belief or evaluation, all within seconds and without your conscious control. This is how your *"system"* of beliefs either imprisons or empowers you both in the present moment and over time. You're at a party or at someone's house or in a work gathering, and someone walks in the room. Within seconds you've formed an evaluation, a *"feeling,"* a judgment. Or your friends stop by and say, *"Hey, we're going skydiving! Want to go?"* Bam! There it is again, making an instant evaluation of whether to accept or decline.

References

The weights on the evaluation scale are placed by many **factors** or **references.** We judge against our own internal set of standards and biases, fears, doubts, confidence level, self-esteem, likes and dislikes. Some of these can dynamically change from moment to moment as new sensory input enters our mind. Even our mood affects our evaluations. One of the best ways to break up a limiting or disempowering belief that's been plaguing you is to **separate your identity** from the belief. Think of beliefs as clothing, as something you wear or put on your body. Your body (who you are) isn't the garment. You have the ability to take off a belief that is disempowering. Start a Perry Mason line of tough questioning on the belief. Put the belief or viewpoint under the spotlight and grill it with tough questions until it no longer has a hold on you.

Truth

I like the analogy that truth is like the center of a town. **There may be different roads to the center of town but you will always end up in the same place.** Truth discovery is enlightening, just as untruth is a form of darkness. And since it is our nature to want to be in the know, we resist and fear the unknown. Our exact version of truth can be different from others' because we all have **rose-colored glasses** that tint our perspectives, as you will see in the next chapter. But those glasses can also affect our beliefs about what <u>we</u> call our reality. **Our collection of beliefs and perspectives defines our reality.** This concept is extremely important in creating change to our "reality" if we don't like it.

"The way I see it…"

Truth Decay

Some of the most debilitating banes of progress are **fear** and **ignorance.** No one is immune, but there are "inoculations" to what I call **"truth decay."** Truth decay means operating under false information or beliefs and then suffering consequences that could have been avoided. We've all had that head-smacking moment of realizing we're headed down a primrose path. When you experience every major breakthrough or life-changing milestone, you take a step away from fear, ignorance, superstition and non-truth. For instance, people once believed that the world was flat and that tomatoes were poisonous. 16th-century geography

154

experts believed California was an island separate from North America. Giordano Bruno and Copernicus helped change false beliefs about the true orientation of the sun.

Tooth decay develops because of a lack of good oral hygiene. Plaque buildup accumulates until its damaging effects are visible. In the same way, *truth* decay doesn't happen overnight. "Plaque" builds up over truth through **neglect**. Neglect often sneaks up on us in the form of laziness, apathy, lack of persistence, or simply getting distracted by another task or life "emergency," and then forgetting to get back to the original task. Thus truth can be distorted by interpretation both intentionally and unintentionally.

Remember the grade school game of "telephone," where one kid whispers a sentence to someone, who then whispers it to the next person, and so on around the room until the last one to hear the message says it out loud? Of course, it's distorted. Asking questions, keeping an open mind about new discoveries and old "truths," does two things for you. First, it keeps you closer to the truth and second, it sharpens and strengthens your belief system, keeping it away from junk. **So what is it that blocks the truth from us?**

"Through ignorance, superstition, prejudice, fear or bias, we may attempt to conceal the truth, but truth doesn't hide; it merely waits to be discovered."

-T. K. Tolman

Certainty—Uncertainty

One thing is certain these days: nothing is certain (or at least many areas of certainty we enjoyed in times past have now faded away). For the purposes of the seven gears, let's call it rust. When any moving metal part gets rusty, it slows down. Like the Tin Man in *The Wizard of Oz*, it comes to a halt because the rust condition is creating more resistance than the original force or power plant can overcome.

The Rust on Trust

Ironically, **one thing we really need IS certainty**. It's a key element of Faith, Hope, and Trust. If ever there was a word that's fallen on hard times, it's got to be the word "trust." It seems that as our modern society moves faster and has unprecedented advantages and technologies, our overall trust of each other, business, and companies has eroded, and with good cause. Jobs and careers change and end more often than they did ten short years ago. Most employees have learned that loyalty and trust are thinner and rarer than in our parents' and grandparents' generations. The blame for this erosion on employee-employer relations does not solely rest on employers. Changes in business survival impacted by rising-falling economic cycles have been a major contributor to the rust of trust.

Overall tensions and anxiety are hacking into our value systems. New prisons can't be built fast enough. State and local governments are now contracting outside services to hold that growing population. Henry David Thoreau's famous words, "Most men lead lives of quiet desperation," seem truer than ever before. It is not my intention to preach on any moral issues; I merely want to say that our value and belief systems are just as important as ever. **And if you truly seek a higher standard of living and quality of life, then strong values, purpose and core beliefs cannot be left out.**

"No accomplishment, no assistance, no training, can compensate for lack of belief."

- Ralph Waldo Emerson

The Four-Part Belief System

Each of us has a number of beliefs and expectations about everything within the Eight Goal Areas. Every belief you have has an **intensity,** or level of strength. Some are steady and unwavering, while others are dynamic and changing, from weak to a full-out conviction. And this is happening every day. For this gear, Faith-Belief, there are **four primary beliefs** that affect the probability of reaching your objectives and putting your best opportunities within reach.

1. Faith-Belief in Yourself

Can You Do It or Not?

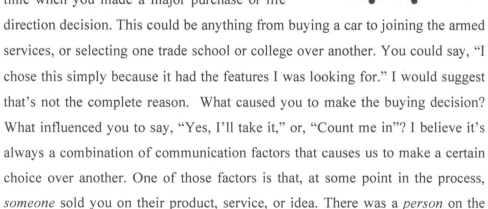

Faith in yourself comes first. Think back to a time when you made a major purchase or life direction decision. This could be anything from buying a car to joining the armed services, or selecting one trade school or college over another. You could say, "I chose this simply because it had the features I was looking for." I would suggest that's not the complete reason. What caused you to make the buying decision? What influenced you to say, "Yes, I'll take it," or, "Count me in"? I believe it's always a combination of communication factors that causes us to make a certain choice over another. One of those factors is that, at some point in the process, *someone* sold you on their product, service, or idea. There was a *person* on the

158

other side of your handshake. That someone could have been a business leader, parent, respected relative or teacher. And that person had confidence in not only their product, but in *himself*. Our buying decisions almost always go to the person who makes us *feel* good or comfortable. We are all emotionally driven decision makers, whether we're buying or selling. This is such an important matter that it qualifies as a key element in Gear 5, Emotion-Feeling, and in Gear 6, Decision-Choice.

Your collective past experiences and your response to those life events are left in your subconscious. How you learned to handle those experiences either reinforced your overall self-esteem or punched holes in it. Today, your level of influence has a lot to do with the amount of confidence you have in yourself. Your level of belief in yourself goes beyond just a feeling; it permeates your entire being and becomes visible in your posture, your face, your breathing, and your liveliness. You must have *faith in yourself* if you are to be inspired enough to act and influence others to get what you want. Faith and belief in yourself is really an attitude that can cause you to succeed over those who may have more "qualifications." Sadly, millions of talented, bright, gifted people allow defeat every day because they lack faith and belief in themselves. People are drawn to those they respect and admire, most of whom have a strong positive self-image combined with a high level of confidence. This is really *faith in themselves* to perform or deliver. Emmy award-winning television producer Roger Ailes expresses it best in his book title, <u>*You Are the Message: Getting What You Want by Being Who You Are*</u>. In the book, Ailes affirms, "You *can* learn to control the time and space you move through, if you really believe in yourself and understand what your mission is in every situation."[35]

At the core of every agreement or negotiation, you bought something or someone because of the faith and belief *they* conveyed. Or on the flip side, someone bought into your idea, product or service because of *your* level of conviction, confidence and faith. Your self-concept is either occupied by faith or fear. The quality of your performance and relationships depend on the internal faith you have **in yourself**. All advancement and growth requires it. You require it. Real faith and belief in yourself is not being arrogant or aggressive because it's not driven by fear-based emotions.

A strong positive belief in yourself gives you:
- ✓ Self-confidence
- ✓ Strength and vigor
- ✓ Improved self-efficacy
- ✓ More control and influence over outcomes and circumstances
- ✓ Better immunity to negative suggestions and thinking
- ✓ Increased odds of winning
- ✓ Improved effectiveness
- ✓ The key to attainment

"If thou canst believe, all things are possible to him that believeth."

(Mark 9:23)[36]

2. Faith-Belief in a Higher Power

It is not the intent of this book to delve into religion except to say that history is loaded with amazing stories and outcomes of those with strong faith in a higher power. If you're serious about making the improvements and changes in the quality of your life experiences then you will not gloss over goal area #6, Mental/Spiritual, as one of your eight core goal areas. We are not here by accident, which means we are here **for a purpose** and reason. We already know that there are things invisible or out of range of our very limited five senses that exist in the subatomic and radio-wave arena. And these energies are much more powerful than what we can see.

There is something inherent in all humans that instinctively knows or senses that there is more to our existence than just being born, living, and then dying. The more we learn about and discover the many marvels in nature and the celestial heavens, the more evidence continues to build that there is an intelligence and power greater than ourselves. Every culture has beliefs in some deity as Creator of all that exists. Alcoholics Anonymous has adopted this Serenity Prayer in their twelve-step program:

> *God, grant me the serenity to accept the things I cannot change,*
> *The courage to change the things I can,*
> *And wisdom to know the difference.*[37]

Faith is incomplete, I believe, if we leave out the Creator, God. My point is that if your Awareness Gear is working, you will become just as attuned to things on a spiritual level as on a mental level. Prayer and meditation are another gift given to us to commune with God, or the Higher Power. Millions will testify to the power of sincere, heartfelt prayer.

3. Faith-Belief in an Opportunity

Some things are self-fulfilling prophecies. The stronger your belief in opportunity and new possibilities coming within your reach, the greater the likelihood of exciting prospects revealing themselves. Recall the cause-and-effect graphic where the cause side contains *any possibility* and *infinite potential*, which means the source of all opportunity. And in Gear 1, we talked about how energy streams where attention beams. Combining the factors of a positive, expectant attitude with a heightened sense of awareness prepares the "soil" for catching new seeds of opportunity. Your belief in opportunities presenting themselves somehow, in some way, activates the principle that what you expect is what you get. And as you will see by the end of this book, this piece, along with the other three faith-belief parts, forms an integrating link through all seven gears.

4. Faith-Belief in a Favorable Outcome, Result, or Condition

At first glance it appears that beliefs one and four are the same thing. Believing in a favorable outcome is really a combination of these belief parts, a mixture of all four reinforcing each other. When you expect the best and see the best in situations, you're creating a "positive outlook" in general. Whenever you undertake a new task or project there's always a sensory level of assurance as you move along, whether or not the end result is achieved. Your level of certainty waxes and wanes as you move toward accomplishment. Some goals or objectives may be abandoned because you reach a point where you don't believe it's going to happen. Other times, you just *know* you're going to get the result you're after. What starts out as hope builds to a level of certainty as you get closer to your target. As we saw in belief area number one, those with dominantly positive expectations actually influence the odds of their success. What we're really talking about here is optimism validated by self-efficacy, a power factor that affects every one of the eight goal areas we defined in the last chapter. Hence the phrase, "success breeds success." What's important to remember is that *you* influence and control the strength of your self-efficacy. It's your belief in your ability to plow through barriers and realize more exciting outcomes that boosts the octane in your fuel to make it happen.

Applying and exercising all 7 gears is how you can fortify these four beliefs into delivering more favorable conditions and experiences. You will create a growing list of successful results, which in turn will strengthen all four of these belief directions. Know that any success, no matter how large or small, is to be counted and used in framing your belief system. The common theme in Gear 3 is the same as it is with all the gears—*you* are the one who shapes and sets the likelihood of realizing more exciting outcomes.

There will always be *outside* events or unpredictable course changes that will get in front of our plans. But the next time a wrench falls into your operating system, it won't have to be a show-stopping event. That's because of the "secret" knowledge you now possess—the knowledge of what you can do between causes and their effects. There are still so-called hands of fate you're dealt according to where you are, who knows you, who you know, what you know or don't know, at what point in time, etc., that create your circle of influence.

Maintaining a strong belief in reaching your goals is not head-in-the-sand thinking when you apply what you've built up in Gear 2 with your Values, Purpose, Goals, and Identity. There's one more benefit these four belief areas give you. Like duck feathers that never get wet, you will gain a sort of Teflon-coating resiliency to better withstand the inevitable barriers, gaps, and diversions you will face along the way. It will take much more to rain on your parade.

Practice doesn't really make perfect, but practicing these four faith-belief parts will increase confidence in your ability to gain more favorable outcomes and results.

163

They will prove themselves to you in the form of goals and desires manifested into the physical realm.

We're just getting started! Wait until you see what's up ahead! You will learn what else you can do to strengthen your internal belief that *you really can* accomplish more favorable outcomes than ever before.

The Collaboration Continuum
Communications Interoperability

When I worked in the field of emergency radio communications, voice and data interoperability was a big deal because police and fire first responders need to be able to communicate voice and data quickly, clearly, and accurately. As obvious as this seems, you'd be surprised at how many agencies are unable to interoperate. It's also amazing how many problems stem from misunderstanding and miscommunication, ranging from little irritating annoyances all the way to war. Mastering what I call **The Collaboration Continuum** can help alleviate the problem of miscommunication.

Your Success Depends on the Support, Cooperation and Goodwill of Others

Every living thing has a relationship with its own kind and its environment. All healthy relationships need effective communication, whether it's in the context of family, business, an organization or association, group-to-group, or one-on-one. There is also a communications continuum between our conscious and subconscious mind.

A person's demeanor and deportment are measured in a rapid process of evaluation and response. Communications feedback signals can flash bi-directionally in milliseconds. NLP practitioners say that the human communication process can be categorized as 38% tonality, 55% physiology, and only 7% through actual words. As complex "transceivers" (transmitter-receiver), we "tune in" to certain nuances, many of which are invisible. Have you ever noticed when someone enters or leaves a room that the chemistry in the air can change? There is a constantly changing energy dynamic with all forms of communication. When you're on the phone discussing a business matter, you can "read" voice tones as feedback. All of these sensory inputs convert to instant evaluations to either move up or down the Continuum, or completely off the grid.

"Life is the business of relationships."

- T.K. Tolman

Building Blocks
of the
Collaboration Continuum

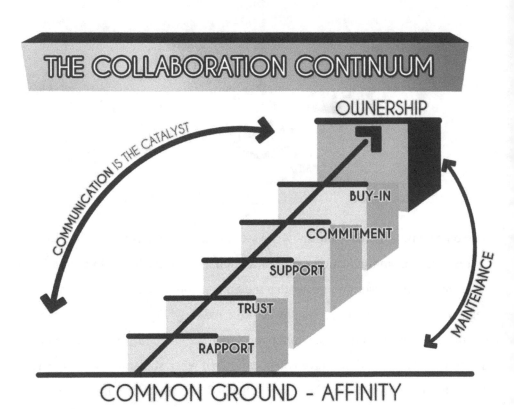

As you can see in the model, **all relationships start at the bottom and evolve up** to the top step of Ownership. If there is any problem with relationships, it can always be traced to failure of one of the stages in the Collaboration Continuum. A person's level of skill and knowledge in the art of communication is critical to success or failure. A person sold on an idea to the level of **Buy-In** can still revert to a lower level if the relationship is not refreshed with mutual benefit, life and activity. Even the best of friends or relatives can move away from each other and correspond less with each passing year. The subject of collaboration and relationship building, be it personal or business, is one that needs much more space and attention than we have here. I will simply say this: **the Collaboration Continuum is the foundation** of make-or-break deals. It's the basis of either good or bad personal and work relationships. This **scale of relational intimacy** works just as well in building personal friendships as it does in keeping marriages happy.

Communication Levels

When a relationship begins, there needs to be a common ground, or an affinity for each other. You meet someone for the first time and discover they have a passion for horses, and so do you! That's **common ground**. Or you hire into a company and are introduced to your coworkers. You have common ground. You may experience a leveling off with one person and stay at that trust level. You have a rapport and you trust them, but that's as far as it goes. You're not interested in supporting or committing to anything beyond the work project you're involved in with that person. Other times you may have totally bought into the idea, product, or relationship, and you're sold, you've got ownership. An interesting thing about taking ownership of a product or deal is that our egos will defend our ownership decisions. Whether it's a friendship, a buying decision, or a tightly held belief, this can be good if what you've bought into and "own" is a positive, empowering thing. But it can also be disempowering if it doesn't serve you or takes you in a direction you don't want to go. Again if your values, purpose, and goals are clear and concise, you should have minimal trouble in this area.

Internal Collaboration

The same thing applies to our line of thinking and beliefs within us. As with many principle-based concepts, some people fall into the working rudiments of this without even being consciously aware of its workings. **Everything runs through a cycle of stages,** and our beliefs run this same gamut. Applying and mastering this model as **a communications guide** will give you a big advantage in your professional and personal life.

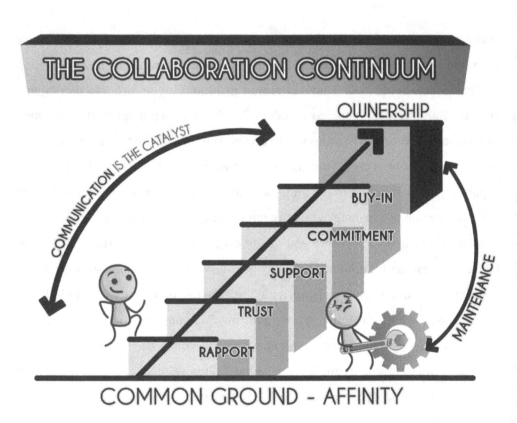

168

Maintenance

The right applications of these steps are, in my opinion, worth millions of dollars in value because your **chances of promotion** or **business opportunities** go up when you use **The Collaboration Continuum** to your benefit. As with any finely tuned running system, the steps require ongoing maintenance and support. You can't reach a level of trust with an associate, for example, and just abandon the original investment steps you took to get to that stage. In other words, **you can't expect trust levels to just sustain themselves**. You can't violate trust or just sit back and do nothing more if you want to keep the trust level up. If you were to reverse viewpoints by thinking from the receiving end, you can quickly see how your trust in someone or something is important. Your client or friendship relationship won't move up the ladder to Support if the trust level is waning. So just remember, using the collaboration continuum can serve you well if you keep communications lines open and if you reinvest in each level continually. Mastering the value of The Collaboration Continuum needs more time and space than this chapter can contain.

Free Will vs. Doubt and Disbelief

The old adage, "A man convinced against his will is of the same opinion still," applies here. We've been told through various religious texts and creeds that we are creatures of free will, and yet are we not prisoners chained by our own disbeliefs and doubts and fears? When the power gear of **Emotion-Feeling (Gear 5),** is attached to **Faith- Belief Gear 3,** this becomes your reality.

The Cinderella Syndrome

As in the tale of Cinderella, we can be kept from going to the ball and our ugly stepsisters (fear, jealousy, discouragement) stand between us and life's great opportunities; the "ball" of life. Except in real life, the barriers holding us back are self-imposed. The key to get out of the locked room is in your pocket. The key is the 7 Gears.

 Limiting, outdated beliefs can block you from experiencing a new, improved outcome reality, and any change in beliefs changes what's possible. An ongoing "worth doing" exercise that applies to all of these gears is to look for and **find working examples of people who have the strong, empowering belief systems** that all winners and champions have. You will make an interesting discovery: all high achievers have a common set of beliefs and faith. None of this is hard to find if you're sincere and really want this gear in your arsenal. I believe you do, or you wouldn't have made it this far. As a booster kit of beliefs, may I suggest adopting some of these time-tested core beliefs of champions and winners?

- Right now, you have one or more built-in talents, skills or abilities that you can excel in
- You're never defeated until you say you are.
- Winners are not born; they're made.
- You have the resources to create your own reality.
- Great success demands great commitment.
- According to your faith and belief will you be, do, and have.

- You are the keeper of your beliefs, and you decide what to keep and what to toss.
- Failure is only a result, and you can use it to advance.
- When you take responsibility, you take control and authority.
- Every adversity contains a benefit, and it can serve you if you find it and apply it.
- You set your level of limitations.

- FEAR
- LIMITING BELIEF
- LOW CONFIDENCE
- ANGER
- JEALOUSY
- NEGLECT
- UNTRUTH
- MISUNDERSTANDING

"Rocks" in Your Backpack Weigh You Down"

We all have our collection of beliefs, some empowering and some disempowering. Those are the rocks that we carry around with us. But we forget that we don't have to carry all those rocks around, and so we just keep carrying our rocks! Yes, they

171

are *our rocks* until the moment you say, **"No more! I'm throwing out these rocks!"** As Dorothy could click her heels anytime and go home, we can choose right now to remove them. You can reduce some of those hardship rocks to manageable pebbles by getting your 7 Gears in working order. English-American poet Edgar Albert Guest offers this perspective on belief and the importance of self-confidence:

> *You can do as much as you think you can,*
> *But you'll never accomplish more.*
> *If you're afraid of yourself, young man,*
> *There's little for you in store.*
> *For failure comes from the inside first,*
> *It's there, if we only knew it,*
> *And you can win, though you face the worst,*
> *If you feel that you're going to do it.*[38]

A Wish Is a Wisp

A wish is the entry-level setting on your potentiometer "volume-power control knob." If level 1 is a "wish" on the energy-power scale, then "commitment" is at the top, the most empowering level, 10. There are differing degrees between full-out conviction and hope. **Commitment is the full-throttle faith** required to get the jet down the runway and off the ground. It's one of the driving forces in the Motivation To Action (MTA) gear set you'll be learning about. **Commitment is where intense desire emotion meets with a decision to go for it!** So if you're going to wish for something, make sure you move up that scale of belief to full-out commitment.

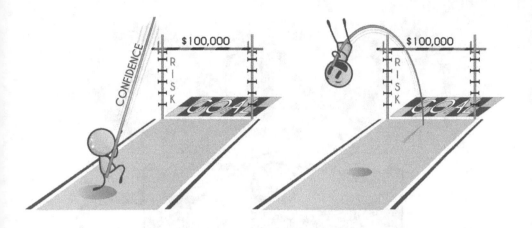

Strong **Faith-Belief** in your goals and purpose gives you pole-vaulting power over barriers, gaps and diversions. **A wish remains a wish unless it has some power behind it.** A wish without power remains a soft idea with a hint of desire. The rays of the sun merely warm an area they shine on, but with concentration like the focusing power of a magnifying glass, they can burn and start a fire. In a locomotive steam engine, if the fire underneath the boiler is just lukewarm, the water above it is merely warmed up, with no steam power. But if the fire heat is turned up enough, steam power is created, and this higher level of power can turn gears and cause wheels to move forward.

To be effective, beliefs and expectations must be conditioned into our subconscious in order to become a part of our Belief System. This conditioning is a mandatory state that all winners and champions possess. And the two best methods are, first, conditioning through **repetition** and **intense emotions (Gear 5).** While we may lose hope in our fellow humans, we must never lose hope in ourselves. Hope, when it's cranked up to the level of conviction, is a full-running gear**, the Gear of Faith-Belief.** And second, we must convert our goal, purpose, and value word statements into the **language that the subconscious will respond to** and accept as orders. This means creating sensory-rich descriptions of each goal, purpose, and value as experiences using all five senses. Not as a bystander looking on, but actually in the experience. If one of your goals is to buy a new car, you would imagine yourself behind the wheel driving it, smelling the new leather, hearing the motor hum, etc. One last thing to keep in mind is that if you try to "force" a result or outcome, it won't work. The conscious and subconscious must be in alignment, and you must translate conscious language to a signal that the subconscious can understand and accept.

Priming Your Wellspring of Opportunities and Ideas

Old versions of well water pumps need to be primed when they're not used for a long time. In other words, water has to be poured down the pump well to get it working again. In the world of economics, governments inject liquid assets in the form of loans and grants into businesses to reactivate the flow of commerce. Similarly, you must **pour some of your efforts** into the well of opportunity; you must first put in the right effort in the right way. Strength, wealth, wellbeing, and more wait in the wellspring of mankind's (your) heritage, ready to be poured out once you learn how to put in the right effort, in the right way. If talent and education do not guarantee success, then what does? The closest thing to a guarantee is unwavering persistence and the full operation of all 7 gears.

We've all heard the common mantra, "You get out of life what you put into it," which is like saying, "you must make a good cake for a good dessert!" What we're talking about here is exactly **what to put into your life-cake** to make it a fabulous experience. Applying the 7 gears gives you the recipe, the formula for living your life on a much more rewarding level. I believe we are all meant to learn the recipe to raise our quality and standard of living. Just like grandma's recipe that's handed down, you model what works. Part of that recipe is that only you can work the well pump to get life's greatest rewards.

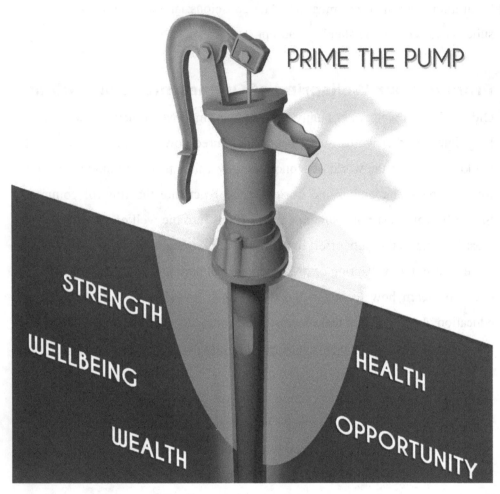

PRIME THE PUMP

STRENGTH

WELLBEING

HEALTH

WEALTH

OPPORTUNITY

Only You Can Work the Well Pump

When you activate and align the 7 gears and systematically apply them in the order and sequence called out in this book, you will be "priming the pump" that taps into the wellspring of exciting opportunities. Every accomplishment carries a price tag, and you must be willing to pay the price for it. The action of "paying the price" should not disturb you if you're sincere about going after the bigger life rewards and a higher standard of living. If you would gain the support and good will of other people, then **find ways to assist others first**. Your success depends on this, and even if your offer is not taken, you still have planted a seed that will benefit you later in some other way in some other place. Refer back to **The Collaboration Continuum** and add to it the **Prime the Pump** principle in order to maximize the combined benefit of these two methods.

Worth Remembering

- Sometimes the best course correction to your goals could be a slight change, not a major alteration.

- Your belief system affects your reality, limited or unlimited.

- Sincere, heartfelt prayer and meditation have been called the "mightiest power in the world." We were meant to communicate with God, our higher power.

- The film of your beliefs develops and projects your version of reality.

- Your level of *applied faith* determines your level of limitations and your number of opportunities.

- Faith and strong belief give you the x-ray vision to see through any temporary setback or defeat.

- "According to your faith be it unto you."

- Strong faith gives you pole-vaulting power over barriers, gaps, and diversions.

- Yes, you do have a special talent or gift, and the world awaits. Faith and belief are strengthened by exercising it and applying it.

- Doubt and belief are the controlling factors of your destiny because they accumulate every waking moment.

- You don't *observe* faith and belief; you *apply* and *internalize* them, IF you want them to really work in your life.

- Your subconscious mind takes orders and delivers those orders according to your emotion-laden belief system.

- What belief-seeds you plant will produce exactly after their kind. What kind are you planting right now?

- Summary: When your <u>Faith-Belief</u> system changes, your outcomes, results and conditions change!

<u>Worth Doing</u>

- Exercise both faith in God or Higher Power *and* yourself as co-pilots. Start with a few short flights, make some test runs, then circle the globe.

- Since each of your beliefs is a choice, choose empowering beliefs.

- The more deeply you internalize your belief, the more you empower your vision to materialize.

- Be intensely focused on your goals but not desperate, because that type of emotion will "throw a rod" in your engine and take you out of the race.

- Strong faith and belief don't eliminate fear; they put it in its place where you can leverage it to your advantage.

- Practice the art of applying more "belief-seeds" in what you can and will accomplish. You've got to plant first in order to harvest

- Don't delay belief until you see it. See it when you believe it!

- You can plant seeds of gratitude right now that will harvest happiness and more.

- Yes, we need rules and regulations, but we also need free-running imagination and forward thinking that challenges status quo and asks, "What if...?"

Your Faith-Belief System, Gear 3,

directs and drives your...

Gear ·4

PERSPECTIVE-VIEWPOINT

"You can become blind by seeing each day as a similar one. Each day is a different one; each day brings a miracle of its own. It's just a matter of paying attention to this miracle."

-Paul Coelho[39]

Paradigm as Viewpoint/Position

Have you ever noticed how a trip to the grocery store looks very different on the way home than it does on the way to the store? You have two differing viewpoints, even if you take the same path. With your viewpoint direction changed 180 degrees, viewing angles and lighting also change so that you're able to see different things. "Paradigm," a popular term in recent times, is identified as a **"perception or frame of reference"** and is an important element in this 4th Gear. Gears 1 and 4 are similar in their makeup in that they both involve the faculties of sensory acuity, be it mental, spiritual, or physical in nature.

The sextant is a tool that's been used for centuries at sea for navigation to help sailors get a fix on their position in order to stay on course toward their destination. As a life navigator, you need to "get a fix" periodically on where you are and which direction you need to go to reach your goals and destination. No one can do this for you. You must be your own captain and navigator. Use this gear and the other supporting gears as your "sextant"—your direction and route finder.

I am always amazed that many people, myself included, lose sight of foundational truths. Often we forget the fact that we are always in charge of our life direction and outcomes because of our gifts of **free will and decision.** Perhaps it has to do with the invisibility of working laws. Our attention is often directed to the present moment's crisis, barrier, gap or diversion. **We get caught up in the present moment, get off focus and lose long-term perspective.** That's what we're talking about here, the critical importance of **Perspective Gear 4.**

Opportunity and perceptions are interrelated. Opportunities present themselves every hour, every day. But are you AWARE of them when they come? Do you recognize the diamond in the "rough" of work and persistence required to follow through? Many opportunities come veiled to the person whose sensory acuity is either dulled or diverted because of apathy or distraction. Opportunities are fluid and always on the move, like floating driftwood on a stream; it comes within our reach and we can grab onto it, but if not acted on, it drifts out of range.

Interactive—Bidirectional

Whenever the subject of change comes up, one of the foundational prerequisites involves **first a change in perception and viewpoint.** When you were a child, did you ever see something hiding in your closet or under your bed? You just *knew* there was something there! And when you tried to explain this to your parents, they told you it was just your imagination. And of course, it was. But in the moment, it was real. From your **perspective**, it was a fact. As you grew older, you came to realize that the "truth" you believed was indeed nothing but your imagination. Right now, today, there are some viewpoints and perspectives you are holding onto that just ain't so! These can be in any area of your life: financial, educational, relational, career, family, home, mental, or spiritual.

Perspectives, viewpoints, and attitudes are closely tied to our belief system. And so when you change one, you cause a change in the other. Because these seven gears are interactive, a change in one alters all the others, just as real gears would. When you have a change of perspective, either an empowering or disempowering one, it will impact your faith, your emotions, your decisions, and even your actions.

Hidden Image Auto-Stereograms

A few years ago, books of novelty picture illusions generated by computers became popular. These pictures are designed to create the impression of a 3D scene from a two-dimensional image. The computer-generated images are made up of horizontally repeating color patterns. The idea is to stare at the flat pattern until at some point, a 3D image *becomes* visible as a dinosaur, dolphins, or whatever the graphic artist created. The image is always there, but only when our discernment *suddenly* "sees" it does it seem to appear. Such are the workings of our attention, awareness, and sensory acuity. If you want to have some fun, look up "stereogram" on Google and test your perception on these clever hidden images.

Ophthalmologists will tell you we all have blind spots with our physical eyes. But a scotoma, as it's called, can also be psychological in the form of a *mental* blind spot characterized as an inability to perceive certain matters. Some of these blind spots brought on by our moods and biases in the moment can also be removed, like cataracts that block our field of vision.

When you alter your viewpoint and perspective, suddenly you tap into the Cause of all possibilities Gear. The amazing thing is that the "new" options and opportunities were always there!

"I say it's a one!"

"No! It's a zero!"

Profound truths and opportunities have similar characteristics. They both seem shy, evasive, and veiled in their first presentation until you "ask" your way into their presence.

We must first
- Be ready, willing, and able to receive and accept;
- Desire them with sincerity;
- Be sensitive and alert to their existence or momentary presence;
- Be respectful and appreciative.

As in the hunt for an elusive butterfly, you must be **deliberate in your approach** and of course, have your net ready.

Turning Points

Turning points are really decision points. These occur at an emotional level that exceeds our predetermined threshold of tolerance. Turning points also come from thinking and viewing something from a different perspective. For example, we've talked about how one of the big causes of low ambition is fear of failure. I mean, who really likes the feeling of failing? And who likes to return for another dose of it? BUT what most people don't **see** is that failure is one of the combinations to open the door of the safe that holds the treasures of life! When you get serious about studying the elements of success in any field, "failure" is always there. A jet plane heading from Denver to New York is off course (failing many times) on its way to its destination. The probability of purchasing a winning lottery ticket is the same as that of achieving **worthwhile** goals without experiencing any failure: one in X million! Putting failure in proper perspective changes our attitude from fear to an empowering, "Bring it!" Viewing so-called failure as a teacher and viewing failure as a character builder can be the defining difference between using your failure, or failure using you.

Failing is Like Rowing

So-called "failure" is like part of the rowing cycle in a canoe; it's merely the temporary point when the oar is up and out of the water before dropping back in and going for another stroke. It's all part of the process of moving forward. One of the most influential automotive engineering geniuses of the last century was Charles F. Kettering. He put in plain words the best way to "fail" smartly: "Keep on going and the chances are you will stumble on something, perhaps when you are least expecting it. I have never heard of anyone stumbling on something sitting down."[40] There is one caveat to this approach to unwanted outcomes: You must learn something, anything, and bring it with you on your next attempt.

Turning points, epiphanies, or a paradigm shift seem to happen suddenly and be unpredictable in their arrival. For some, the trigger can be a book, for others a song or something someone says, even if unintentionally. It could be what you hear in the news or something you encounter in your network of friends, associates or relatives. Interestingly, what gets a turning point off the launch pad and into orbit is a highly emotional moment, either positive or negative. The unique combination of factors and conditions are often what lead up to this transition, but ultimately, the actual change point happens in a moment.

Paradigm Shift and Paradigm Drift

In the business world, almost everything revolves around projects. There are a number of project protocols and even certifications dedicated to project facets and skills. One thing that commonly plagues project managers is trying to stay on time and on budget. A project off course for any reason has "scope creep." The project *drifts* off course for any number of reasons. It must be dealt with quickly, or disaster is imminent.

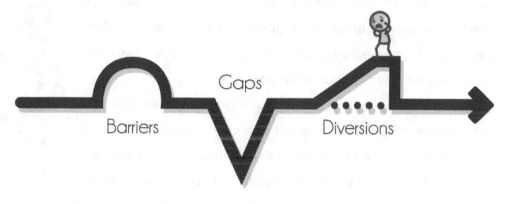

Diversions

Diversions from our goals and objectives can pull us off course. Over the last 20 years, there's been much discussion about paradigms. The significance of a paradigm shift, or having an "epiphany," has much to do with our perspectives and viewpoints. However it's been characterized, it still is worth mentioning here because viewpoints and perspectives on any subject can create a bias that can either be empowering as a vantage point or disempowering as fear. And let's get real here, everyone has biases and prejudices, everyone. Unfortunately, many are not of good value and don't serve us well.

Attitude Shapers and Life-Quality Makers

Questions Shape Our Perspective and Viewpoints

Questions do more than start you on your way to an answer, **they control and direct your attention.** Questions are a perception tool that can get you pointed in the right direction or pull you down like a boat anchor. Author Tony Robbins often says, "Quality questions create a quality life."[41] The way a question is framed can make all the difference in serving you with best solutions and high-quality ideas. **Well-framed questions sharpen and strengthen your values, goals, purpose, and identity.** After reading this chapter, return to Gear 2 armed with this information and upgrade your Values, Purpose, Goals and Identity declarations.

As light energy overcomes darkness, so also can positive emotions, perspectives, beliefs and viewpoints override uncertainty. One of the quickest ways to turn the tide away from the darkness of ignorance and limitation is to begin the empowering habit of asking good questions. The importance of well-framed questions is overlooked by so many because they don't understand how much they influence our outcomes and experiences.

Questions "Throw the Stick"

Questions "throw the stick" to "go fetch" and bring back answers. One of the greatest information-age revolutions has come about from combining Internet technology with computers, creating exponential access to the largest knowledge base in history. Unprecedented asking power now exists with super information access systems such as Google and Wikipedia. Getting excellent answers depends on excellent questioning. Asking questions is like putting a key in a lock. Answers are really a collection of responses, and responses are effects, and results. Answers also work within the Law of Cause and Effect, a vantage point that can serve us.

The "Big Six" Viewpoint Framers

Every question you ask runs through these pointers: **who, what, when, where, why, and how.** When you point any question through these six perspectives, you get six different answers. Purposeful directing of a question through these six angles will net you bigger, better, more useful answers. Once again, the benefits of this technique are often overlooked.

1. *Who* you ask—yourself, God, other people, the internet
2. *What* you ask
3. *When* you ask a question—timing
4. *Where* you ask a question—books , videos, friends, neighbors, work associates, relatives, social networks
5. *Why* you're asking; in what context, and for what purpose
6. *How* you shape the question, and *How* many questions you ask

Now here's the tricky part. Simply making a point to ask is most beneficial, but how you *frame the question* is what makes the BIG difference!

It's easy to forget that **presupposed negative questions will get you negative answers** just as quickly and thoroughly as positively framed questions will return positive, forward-moving answers! Once again, this universal truth gets lost in the dust because we don't realize its power to take us where we want to go!

Idea-Sparking Generator from Questions

The flint that ignites the fuel of any possibility runs through **The Big Six** questions. Question asking can be empowering or disempowering depending on *how* you ask, *what* and *when* you ask, and even *whom* you ask. What you *don't* ask can get you different and biased answers. There are good questions and bad questions just based on how you word the question. Questions like, "Why do I always get the short end of the stick?" or, "Why can't I ever get a break?" will always return a lousy answer. If you ask an empowering question such as, "Why do I always find good deals when car shopping?" you will get one or more answers that give supporting evidence! It's the old axiom, "Garbage in, garbage out." **Stop right now and ponder the significance of this!** This is one example of how our subconscious mind takes our conscious orders and finds answers.

I'm always amazed at how Jeanette, my wife, gets better rental car deals and better airfares just by asking. We once got one of the top hotel rooms at the fabulous Rock Resorts in Vail, Colorado, for $60 a night, even though it normally went for $700 a night, just because of the way she asked! And one time on a trip to Honolulu, my six-year-old son took off into the crowd at Waikiki beach, asking every kid, "Would you play with me?" He moved on undeterred when families told him to shove off and went to the next group of kids. It absolutely worked; he made all kinds of friends just by asking—enough times.

Questions and answers are the rungs to knowledge, skill, and wisdom.

The More You Ask, the More You Get

- **Good questions get you good answers and solutions.**
- **Bad questions get you bad answers.**
- **Questions that challenge bad assumptions can cause changes and turning points.**

Here is an example to help in framing a question that gives you what you need, even if the answer is not what you expected. Let's run it through **The Big Six**:

Objective: "I want to increase my income by 10%."

- **What do <u>I need to change</u> in order to go in the direction I want?**
- **<u>Who can I meet with or talk to</u> or read about that gives me the answers I seek?**
- **<u>When should I move</u> on this?**
- **<u>Where can I go</u> to get options and things I need to do?**
- **<u>Why do I want this</u> so much?**
- **How can I <u>get this financial situation turned</u> around ASAP?**

And here is an example of challenging a bad assumption to cause changes and turning points:

Bad Assumption: "I will *never* get to travel to Paris."

- According to **WHOM**?
- **WHY** never? Really, honestly, never, ever, ever?
- But *if I could* – **HOW** could I make it happen?

- **WHAT** plan *could* I come up with?
- **WHERE** can I start a *different approach* to find a way to get to Paris?
- **WHEN** could I *take the first step* to make this goal happen?

When couched in a positive way, the **Big Six** question framer will return you answers that can give you traction on moving forward with your objective or challenge.

Questions have the power to turn you away from negativity in an instant. *Positively framed questions* can quickly turn you way from negativity. Try this question on your spouse or significant other: "Why am I so lucky to have you?" Now you've got to be sincere, of course, but watch how this generates a "warm glow" moment that feeds a series of even more related, positively structured questions. Later in this chapter you will see the empowering effects gratitude can have in shaping your viewpoint and perspective. Remember what we said earlier about asking more "how" questions than "if" ones. Just make sure you end it in a positive tone.

Now More Than Ever

Today, we all have access to the entire planet's untold wealth of online information through search engines and mobile apps. All of this for free! Even if you don't have a computer or smart phone, you can still walk into any library and gain access to anything about everything! The point is, **there are no excuses for not accessing answers that can help you** get the knowledge to move ahead faster in any of your eight goal areas.

If we believe something to be true or not true, we draw upon our *attitude program bank* to form an instant perspective or viewpoint. Many times our convictions of a "truth" may be totally off base and incorrect.

The 2nd Gear, Blueprint-Operating System, begins forming during our early years. As impressionable young kids, we are easily programmed and conditioned. Beliefs and attitudes are picked up from preachers, teachers, relatives, parents, and schoolmates without doubt or question. But as we grow older, we sometimes begin to doubt what we've been told. As it is in the physical world, we cannot hold a complete positive attitude when doubt exists in the inner mind. Like an old-fashioned slide projector, we can hold only one attitude at a time. And while there are varying degrees, it's either positive or negative. This is a very important point in learning what factors we do have control over, because after all, isn't that what we're trying to figure out?

Obstacles on Your Runway Block Your Takeoff!

Rocks of Resentment, Dwelling on Past Hurts, Fear of Failure, Apathy, Disbelief

When coming upon an obstacle, your approach is set by your frame of mind, your *perception*, and your *viewpoint*. Most of these "rock-blockers" are self-generated, which means YOU are the one who needs to get them off your runway to progress! One interesting benefit about barriers, gaps, and hurdles is that when you finally do get through to the other side, you have a knowledge bit that you've earned to take with you as you move on, building **a bank account** of Knowledge, Skill and Future Ability. The cash value could be worth millions to you later on. As Andrew Carnegie said, "…every failure carries with it, in the circumstance of the failure itself, the seed of an equivalent advantage."[42] Some decision paths, however, you would do well to not go down, no matter what the price. When you find yourself in a questionable situation, ask yourself, "Is this serving me? Is the value of this experience worthy of my time?"

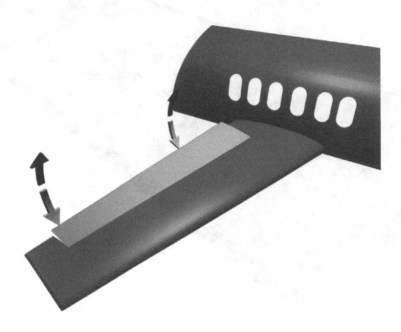

Climbing or Diving – <u>You</u> Control Your Attitude Flaps

Zig Ziglar said, "We can alter our lives by altering our attitudes."[43] Before an airplane takes off, the pilot will adjust and set its wing flaps to direct the airflow so that when sufficient thrust is applied, the set of the wing flaps and tail flaps will create lift. Our **viewpoints and perspectives** function in the same way. The setting of the flaps can put us in a downward tailspin or allow us to climb higher and higher. What's important to remember is that the **"attitude flaps" are always at our control.** Airplanes always encounter updrafts (a string of good fortune), and down drafts (a series of bad happenings). Pilots simply adjust accordingly because both are temporary and don't put the aircraft in any real danger. Similarly, we will always encounter a series of updrafts and down drafts, and while updrafts can be windfalls of good fortune, down drafts don't have to be devastating if our attitude flaps are set correctly. Our perspective or perception of anything has a huge impact on our belief system and on our feelings and emotions (the next gear).

Who doesn't love the classic Dr. Seuss story, *How the Grinch Stole Christmas*? Remember how his attitude and viewpoint changed when he heard the music continuing on down in Whoville, and his heart grew larger? Remember the famous Charles Dickens story about Scrooge and the transformation of his stingy viewpoint? And what about Phil Conner, played by Bill Murray in the film *Groundhog Day*, who changed his viewpoint and had an impact on the whole town of Punxsutawney as a result of his changed perspective? Even though the stories are fictional, the parables they demonstrate are spot-on in presenting the real magnitude of viewpoint changes.

Viewpoint **changes can happen in the moment; they don't have to take days and years,** although there may be preparatory conditions leading up to the instant decision. Thinking back on your own life-altering experiences, weren't there times when you had an instant change in viewpoint? It could have been something a trusted friend said to you, or witnessing or experiencing a tragedy or negative event. These changes in perspective may seem insignificant or imperceptible in the moment, but their long-term impact can cause **huge differences** for better or worse later on.

Radiation Poisoning

Negative attitudes are like radiation poisoning. If you are exposed to a damaging amount of radioactive material or excessive sun exposure, the damaging effects

201

may not show up until much later. Weeks, months, or even years may pass until the harm reveals itself. <u>Treat chronically negative people as "radioactive" and stay clear from "exposure" to them</u> because the damaging effects may not show up for months or years. That "damage" could show up, for example, in a discouraged person unable to see an opportunity today because of years of negative influence from a well-meaning but ignorant associate or relative.

Have you ever experienced a bad situation with a negative boss or poor teacher? There's nothing special about it – they're out there, and you will cross paths with one sooner or later. Hold the viewpoint, *"How can I learn from this unhappy or painful experience?"* These types of people can be used as **"anti-mentors."** The uncomfortable, unforgettable experience can fire your emotions enough to make sure you never are like that, which ironically sharpens your Value System. Some of my most motivating experiences have come from working with extremely negative people. Any experiences that clash with your Values and Identity will spark you to improve the situation—IF your self-esteem and self-image are strong and healthy. Sometimes you're locked in a work arrangement with excessively negative coworkers and can't get away from them. If the job is still worth it and has more positives than negatives, then think of yourself as *Teflon*® or rubber coated, refusing to let any negatives stick on you. It sounds silly, but it actually works if you make it fun and practice it. You always want to take command of excessive negative talk by simply changing the subject, even if it's obvious and you can't get away. Do this enough times and the "**negatron-bomber**" will get the message and move on to other, more willing "ain't it awful" club members. As the Peter McWilliams book title suggests, *You Can't Afford the Luxury of a Negative Thought*.

Two or More

A change in perspective or viewpoint often involves two or more pieces of information:

- 2 or more facts or truths
- 2 or more non-truths
- Observations or experiences, either positive or negative
- Questions you ask
- Questions you don't ask
- Questions you got an answer for
- Comparisons and contrasts.
- 1 or more truths hidden among non-truths
- 1 or more non-truths hidden among truths

Any one of these information inputs may be delivered by another person or group, or from yourself.

Fact or opinion + Evaluation/judgment + Attitude (positive or negative) = Viewpoint: Positive (empowering) or Negative (disempowering)

When I worked as a radio systems engineer for Motorola, one of my jobs was to set and build radio towers for various businesses. There is a structural engineering rule that requires plumbing, or setting a plumb line on the foundational piece, or using a level. In this case, the first section of radio tower is then set in concrete. If that first section is even one quarter of an inch off, it will create an error of being crooked by several inches, depending how high the tower is. Early childhood and teenage foundational viewpoints and perspectives that might be slightly off can have the same multiplied effect later on.

Sharpen Your Decision-Making Ability

Mature, positively framed attitudes give you better decision-making ability. A positive viewpoint can give you a better vantage point than negative perspectives because most negative viewpoints are limiting and restrict your awareness of newer and better insights. With new insights, you rise above petty, unimportant issues or challenges that would otherwise bog you down like one of those "rocks" in your backpack. You increase the odds of tapping into better opportunities.

As-SUMP-tions

In certain areas, homes that have a high probability of collecting excess water in their basements and crawl spaces have **sump** pumps installed to remove excess water that can damage foundations and create mold. Wrong as**sump**tions can collect excess "water" and cause "moldy" damage to **our ability to think and reason clearly** if not cleaned out from time to time. Assumptions can be dangerous because they contaminate your belief system by an **untrue belief** or by **distorted prejudice**. Assumptions can also take you off course without your awareness, resulting in wasted time and effort and setting you back in expense. Asking timely questions can act as a sump pump to remove "stinkin' thinking." Even if you don't run through the Big Six, simply asking what's working and what's not working can help keep excessive assumptions from damaging your forward-moving progress.

The Bane of Today's Workforce

When making decisions, **never assume** anything if there could be important consequences. To reiterate, the best antidote to foolish assumptions is to **ask questions**. Wrong assumptions cause unwarranted relationship anxiety. Working under the guise of clearly defined roles, **misunderstanding and wrong assumptions are one of the big problems in the work force today**. A surprising number of people don't have a clear understanding of exactly what their manager or supervisor really wants. "Oh, I thought you meant you wanted it this way!" says the frustrated employee. Just one clarifying question can save a lot of grief later on. As odd as it sounds, many people would rather keep quiet and not expose their ignorance (as the saying goes), than speak up and remove all doubt. We saw earlier how to eliminate this problem with the Collaboration Continuum. Remember in the Introduction, we talked about how most challenges in every industry come down to 80% about human interoperations and 20% about the technology, no matter how hi-tech a company is.

The Life-Enhancing Principle of Gratitude

The importance and value of a constant state of honest gratitude cannot be over emphasized; it's that important! Having an "attitude of gratitude" about as many heartfelt things as you can sincerely come up with accomplishes a number of value-added enhancements to this gear. Believe it or not, holding this Perspective-

Viewpoint is one of the first prerequisites to building wealth and prosperity. In *The Science of Getting Rich*, Wallace D. Wattles says of gratitude, "The mental attitude of gratitude draws the mind into closer touch with the source from which the blessings come."[44] If you use your **1st Gear, Attention,** to dwell on negative and bad things, then you will find yourself *magnetizing* more negative and unhappy circumstances. Focusing on what you're grateful for points your mind to the better things, strengthening your **Faith and Belief Gear 3**, which in turn enhances the smooth running of the remaining gears. **Focus on what you ARE grateful for. Starting RIGHT NOW, RIGHT HERE!**

Again, it's important to be sincere, humble, and consistent. You must think beyond the big gifts and **be thankful for even the little things**. I've discovered that many of those little "insignificant" things are hidden gems of much value, much larger than first thought. You can prove this by thinking back to a seemingly insignificant event in your past, and with 20/20 hindsight, you see how important and even life-changing it was. It could have been a person showing up in your life or a decision you made not to leave the house when you were going to. Everyone has some remembrance of a quirky event that advanced their career or romance, or bypassed an accident. There is a Law of Increasing Abundance contained in the Law of Cause and Effect. When your thankfulness goes up, so does your abundance level!

As odd as it sounds, even unpleasant events and conditions, including temporary setbacks and failures, are worth being thankful for. Painful events and experiences put in proper context can be hugely profitable by giving you wisdom in the form of a lesson that you can benefit from. One last thing about gratitude and thankfulness; don't just keep it in inside; humbly express to others just how thankful you are. Make an everyday habit of expressing thankfulness in three directions: **past, present, and future**. "Thank you for what you've given me in the past, what I am receiving now, and what is on its way!"

You will see later on the importance and value of developing powerful daily action habits. This is one of them because it strengthens your faith and it keeps your perspectives in the positive. This is one of those secrets of why: **"To those who have, more will be given."**

Changing your attention and focusing on something, anything you're thankful for, is one of the best antidotes to the poison of envy and jealousy. It also strips away any petty complaints you may have about how bad things are. **There is always something you can be grateful for.** It's estimated that 40% of the world's population does not own a pair of shoes. And the U.S. Children's Bureau reports that nearly 400,000 children are in foster care, most of these children brought in because of physical and sexual abuse, neglect, and abandonment. So be thankful for things like your eyesight, the privilege to be here on life's journey, the clothes on your back, and how really, really good you have it compared to those in third-world countries.

The "Be-Attitudes"

Remember the BE-Attitudes

Be-lieve – You can reach your goals; you are here for a positive, life-contributing purpose.

Be-cause – That's *purpose* – the reason you're doing it

Be-g**in** – Starting is half done; to begin means you're **in.**

Be-ware – Of **dis**empowering habits or distractions that can gradually pull you off course.

Be-long – to something bigger than yourself.

Years ago, personal development pioneer Earl Nightingale made a recording called "Lead the Field." Nightingale reveals, "When you begin to develop a better attitude, you realize that you've already placed yourself among the top five percent of the people – among the most successful people on Earth."[45] A positive or negative attitude acts as a *pointer* as to which direction and latitude your perspective and viewpoint are aimed.

"A smooth sea never made a successful sailor."

– Herman Melville

Journaling—Perspective Shaper

On Paper or Electronic Journaling Again

Earlier we learned about the value of journaling in shaping and enhancing your **Operating System,** revealing your true values and intentions, and looking back on wisdom gained on your goal setting adventure. Another empowering viewpoint shaper is having a journal or journal section **dedicated only to things you are grateful for.**

There's something about writing that **sharpens your focus** and **clarifies your thinking**. Having a growing list of anything and everything you are thankful for is a great tool in enhancing and sharpening viewpoints that can serve you. It can really help you gain an accurate perspective of just how rich you are, no matter what your bank account says. I was having this discussion with a friend recently, and he said, "I can't think of anything to be grateful for!" I replied, "You have 20/20 vision, don't you?" He said, "Well, yeah, so what?" I asked if he realized how valuable and fortunate he was to have good vision. Most valuables, if you think about it, are not material possessions. If you live in a free world country, you should always, be grateful for the freedoms you have. Be grateful for your military protection that continues on. Never forget the price paid for your level of freedom today.

Power Framing vs. The Box

I'm sure by now you've heard the cliché, "think outside the box." Your "box" has been under construction since you were a toddler. Boxes formed from rules, regulations, and restrictions have contributed to your present-day belief system. Remember as a kid how fun it was to play with boxes, just plain old boxes? Why was it so fun? Because as children, our imaginations and beliefs are still forming and at that wonderful life stage, anything we can dream up seems possible. Whether the box was an airplane cockpit, a rocket, or a princess castle, in that moment, you really could see it, feel it, **experience** it, and **believe** it! Then what happened? We grew up. Our circle of authority figures orders us to grow up, get real, snap out of it, and get our heads out of the clouds! And so the beginning of **the other kind of box** begins to form, the **box of limitation, security, control**, bolstered by a series of **disappointments.** Obviously, I'm not advocating abandoning government rules and regulations. We need those for civil order and public safety. I'm talking about personal development rules and beliefs and how they can help or hinder tapping our potential if they're not upgraded as we grow in maturity. Nevertheless, isn't it interesting that now, as working adults, we are told, "You've got to think *outside* the box!" The concept of power framing would have you upgrade your "box" and use rules, laws, and truths that empower and accelerate you toward your goals. It is time to get out of the old box mindset. That is what the 7 Gears is about.

Rose-Colored Glasses and Tinted Window Panes

Recall that we touched on the rose-colored glasses concept and its effect on our Belief System. When it comes to **Viewpoints** and **Perspectives,** we all see the world with a set of colored lenses. These lenses are "colored" with **biases** that affect our viewpoints. For example, a person's ego can block clear vision or clinch a belief from past experiences, conditioning or training. We all have a customized set of views of the world or global perspectives. The thing to be aware of is that these colored lenses can **distort reality.** No one is totally free of their colored viewing lenses. Of course, **these lenses aren't real except that the one who is looking through them says they are.**

In the workplace, these differences can cause difficulty in the interactive communication process. If you ever want to get past a person's lenses, you have to learn what his **shade of biases** are. Asking someone's opinion and viewpoint will reveal where his biases are. Look for evidence of what's important to him by outward preferences in clothing style, office or home decorations, and pictures. All of these can give you a better understanding of that person's **perspective and belief lenses.** Since people love to express their opinions, asking key questions about his outlook on any subject can be quite revealing on what **shade** his lenses are. Get good at this skill, and it will serve you well by giving you a one-up vantage point on any negotiations.

The Daily Dozen Train of Thought

One of the most useful tools I've discovered is what I call "the daily dozen." These are 12 outlook-altering memories. Think of them as **imaginary reference boxes,** cubbyhole compartments, or go-to places that can reenergize you, re-center you, or simply reset your perspective about what's important to you. They all give you that "warm fuzzies" feeling. It doesn't have to be 12; you can start with three, two, or just one, but I would recommend building up to at least six. What matters is what these "units" do for you. One of these items could be an actual object. You probably have one right now sitting on your desk that serves as a linking reminder of some pleasant event or memory. It could be **a picture** of your daughter's piano recital, or your son in a Cub Scout uniform, or a picture of you and your friends on top of Pike's Peak, or hearing the song "Fun, Fun, Fun" by the Beach Boys. You could have a **pewter winner's cup** for leading division team sales last year. We all lose our perspective in certain areas of our life from time to time, or we get caught up in a situation at work or home and hit a barrier, gap, or diversion. When you can't take a walk or do something physical in the moment, use these units as quick go-to places. Author Rhonda Byrne calls it the "secret shifter."[46] Others have referred to one's "happy place."

One other suggestion that can add oomph to this technique is to include something that makes you laugh, like **a joke** that stays with you or **a funny scene** in a movie or book, or even **a funny experience** you had that makes you giggle when you recall it. You can amplify the impact by including **favorite smells** (coffee in the morning), **sounds** (wind through the trees/ocean waves), or **feelings** (getting into bed after a long day), anything that makes it a sensory-rich experience. Again, the purpose of this daily dozen is to create an instant change in your present state if it's low. It can also serve as an internal **morale booster** that only you know about.

The following are some examples of what you might place in your numbered reference spaces:

Unit 1 – one or more <u>favorite verses or poems</u>: *"...all things are possible when..."*

Unit 2 – a <u>funny event</u> at work: *When Derek farted in the business meeting.*

Unit 3 – Dad's <u>encouraging words</u> at my graduation.

Unit 4 – the <u>song</u> "Happy" by Pharrell Williams or "Rise" by Herb Alpert

Unit 5 – a <u>powerful thought:</u> *"Every single result that you experience in life is dictated by your habits"*

Unit 6 – A <u>scene from the movie</u> *Airplane* or *Groundhog Day*

Place your daily dozen on your phone, tablet or notebook, or any place you can access it on demand. The beauty of this tool is that it's dynamic and always at arm's length. You can change it and update your entries anytime something better comes along or you're not getting the feel-good effect you once had.

Another Hidden Secret?

Where do you go to get the real kind of change you're after? You've clarified your values, purpose, and goals. You've gotten clear on your identity and upgraded your commitment to exercise your faith. Now what? Is there another "hidden" secret to launching the magnitude of change you must have to make it all work?

Come back from the future and <u>be happy first</u>. Now before you roll your eyes, hear me out. In order to *begin* a change, it must happen in the *present moment*. Changes in your **viewpoint, attitude,** or **belief** must begin *in the now*. You will see this demonstrated later with the Action Wheel making sparks. I first struggled with this life-changing principle because I just couldn't see how that was possible, especially when I was feeling down. Now, I know we can't be on top of the world every waking moment, but we can level out the rollercoaster ride and minimize the depth of the down times. Saying, "Give me the money first, then I'll be happy," is as crazy as saying "Manifest my goal first, then I'll take the steps!" This has been referred to as the "heat-before-the-wood-and-spark syndrome." Here's what you can do to make this work.

First, use your **daily dozen** as a go-to place and pick something that you already listed. Second, go to your **gratitude journal** and relive one of those moments. As suggested earlier, the beauty of these tools and techniques is that with today's mobile technology, you can have it all at your fingertips on your phone. Third, **put these two together,** and something in there should spark that first good feeling. *Now your kindling should be ignited.* This is not living in the past, but rather quickly using past positive references to build your *perspective* and *viewpoint* in the most empowering way to better serve you in reaching your goals. If done properly, these references will become a positive conditioning process. I suggest you update and change out different references as newer, more impactful things come along. Keep it fresh; keep it updated.

Flexibility—Agility

When we look at people with good health and vitality, we see that in addition to having strength and muscle tone, they also have *flexibility* and are *agile*. In the animal kingdom, survival depends on it. Just as there is physical agility, <u>there is great value in having mental flexibility</u>. This means not being too judgmental, having an open mind to other people's ideas and perspectives, and being open-minded in general. You want to be like a bouncing rubber ball, flexible and resilient enough to bounce back from unwanted outcomes or defeats. It also means being flexible about options and possibilities. The human body is healthier when it's flexible and resilient, and it has fewer bones broken or injuries. **Be clear about the goal, but flexible about the ways and means** of getting there.

Have You Opened All Your Presents?

Have you ever observed toddlers opening birthday or holiday presents? They often become enthralled with the wrapping paper and would stop there if not prompted to keep opening their present. Because of our hectic schedules and other distractions, we too can lose sight of our God-given gifts and attributes by forgetting the life-changing, life-directing endowments we've been given. Many times, we can't look past the "wrapping paper."

In addition to the ultimate gift of life, here is a micro sample of the gifts you have in your possession right now:

- ✓ As a free-will agent, you've been given the ability to choose your *direction* and quality of life, including your values as an adult.
- ✓ You've been given the *ability to choose* your response to any and all of your events and circumstances.
- ✓ With your incredible, underutilized mind (processing computer), you can learn and grow through observation, experiences, and modeling best examples to improve and advance in any area of your life, at any time in life.
- ✓ The gift of your ability to *think and reason*
- ✓ The gift of your ability to *visualize and create*
- ✓ The gift of freedom from the shackles of animal instinct, something other life forms don't possess
- ✓ The gift of your capacity for love and good fellowship
- ✓ The gift of your ability to retain and recall good memories and experiences

✓ **The gift of your ability to read, study and learn any subject at any depth and level, and to go as far as you want to go**

✓ **The gift of life and the ability to commune with God, your Creator**

✓ **The gift of six senses to experience all of creation**

✓ **If you live in a free world country, freedom to choose your career path and participate in your country's treasures and free enterprise, a very expensive gift.**

Hopefully you've gotten past the "wrapping paper" to open and use your gifts! And since you're not a toddler, you have a responsibility to give thanks for all of your gifts. Make a point of keeping your "gifts" in good working order. As the saying goes, "Use it or lose it." This section could just as easily be in the Gear 6 chapter on Decision-Choice, because what we are really pointing out here is the magnificent, God-given gift of **freedom of choice**. This overlaps on Gear 1, Attention-Awareness, in that we can get caught up in life's diversions and lose sight of this wonderful, powerful gift of choice. It's important to know that these "presents" can be abused and neglected to the point of being taken away from us.

Catherine Ponder's books are worth picking up because she brings a perspective on "prosperity" that other life researchers don't. In her book *Open Your Mind to Receive*, she brings to light that, "there are no straight lines in your growth or to your good. Everything moves in Cycles, both in time and space. Regardless of the number of breaks that appear in the lines of your life, growth is taking place."[47]

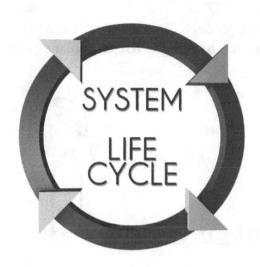

Streams and Rivers Don't Flow in a Straight Line

Streams and rivers don't flow in a straight line; wouldn't it be boring if they did? Such are our life experiences, with twists and turns, rapids and deep still places. Water that is stagnating and has no flow is dead. This is why we should never be bored or apathetic, and if we are, that should serve as a red alert that we are losing precious lifetime. Being bored is a dead water state, a place you don't want to be.

To sum up, viewpoints control our emotions and feelings (next gear, Feeling-Emotion), which then affects our motivation level to act, which drives the 7th **Gear, Action,** which in turn impacts our outcomes or results!

This chapter's Worth Remembering and Worth Doing offer an antidote for discouragement

Worth Remembering

- Gear 1, *Attention-Awareness,* is related to Gear 4, *Perspective-Viewpoint.* Where attention is concentrating, listening or observing something through your six senses, *Perspective-Viewpoint* is when you form a judgment and evaluation of the relative significance and importance of what's being observed according to your own biases and beliefs.

- Think from this perspective: what would your mentor do with the challenge facing you right now? What would your ultimate best self, in top form, do?

- We are, in the present moment, the sum of our negative and positive viewpoints and perspectives.

- If our "attitude scale" takes on more negatives, then fear, doubt, and uncertainty choke off any progress. Tilting in the positive opens up favorable abilities.

- Time, thoughts, and ideas are your irreplaceable life currency. How are you spending and investing them? You don't really "buy" time because your purchase order is set, but you can invest, gain interest and compound the value of your time-life chips.

- Different viewpoints open the "safe" of new opportunities; they were always there waiting to be discovered!

- Stay mindful of your gifts, and be on the lookout for more, because you DO have more, more than you can use!

- Your internal viewpoints and perspectives are powerful enough to affect your health and wellbeing.

- Locked-in perspectives and viewpoints can restrict your opportunities and put you back in the proverbial box. A closed mind to new and different ideas and possibilities is like a clenched fist: you receive nothing, you grasp nothing, and you stay on the bottom rung.

- Keeping an active journal of experiences and insights sharpens your thinking and improves your decision-making ability.

- The more you think in long-term perspectives, the wiser your short-term decisions will be.

- **Summary: When your <u>Perspective-Viewpoint</u> changes, your experiences and conditions change.**

Worth Doing

- Don't say to yourself, "I failed;" say, "I missed the mark or came up short *this* time. Now what's the lesson I just paid for?" Mr. Mistake can be a great teacher with much value if you're open to using the lesson you just paid for.

- Start your "Daily Dozen" list of good feeling memories, songs, poems, movies, books, presentations, or speeches. The laughter and good feelings you get from Your "Daily Dozen" can be a great inoculation to the debilitating viruses of negativity and "thought rot."

- Make a point of asking more questions around the "Big Six" and be pleasantly surprised at your new-found options and opportunities!

- Be agile enough to be able to laugh at yourself and chalk up any mistakes as part of the game of life.

- Overcome the infamous fear of rejection and any self-imposed bad feelings by keeping the long-term perspective as stepping stones to success.

- If your financial goal of, say, $120,000/year seems too daunting, break it up and think of $30,000 every quarter or $2,300/week. Divide and conquer.

- View every problem as a fun challenge for growth and learning.

- Be sincerely thankful for *everything* in your life if you're serious about experiencing the Law of Increasing Abundance.

- Reactivate your childhood curiosity. It served you then; it can serve you today. Just try it for a week and see what happens.

- Get as much laughter and good feeling out of your "Daily Dozen" as possible. Grow it, build it, and upgrade it if any unit stops working for you or if you find something new and better to add. You might get on a roll and go past 12!

Your Perspective-Viewpoint Gear 4

drives and affects your...

Gear •5

EMOTION-FEELING

*"The energy of emotion and feelings can be harnessed like sled dogs
to pull you forward when you are in command."*

- T.K. Tolman

The Energy of Emotion

The power of strong emotions and feelings is the *primary muscle*, the primary force that delivers the power to turn the ACTION GEAR. Best-selling author Tom Hopkins puts it eloquently in his must-read classic, *The Official Guide to Success:* "The emotions are the motors that power the changes you want to make happen. The keener you make yourself feel those emotions, the quicker they'll do their work."[48]

Emotion has its own energy. Remember, the fundamental law of energy is that energy can neither be created nor destroyed; it can only be **transformed** from one type to another. Energy as we know has many different forms: thermal (heat), chemical, potential, electrical, kinetic, electrochemical, electromagnetic, sound, and nuclear. Why are we discussing energy here? It is not my intention to give a science lesson on the differing forms of energy, but this does pertain to the energy of human emotion in the context of the 7 Gears.

Emotions Can Empower or Imprison

Our **emotions have energy,** and any form of energy creates a force field effect. Our emotions contain a type of fuel that can be used and consumed constructively or destructively. Gasoline contained and expended inside a well-engineered engine creates forward-moving power. That same gasoline ignited in a house or forest can also be destructive. Likewise, our emotions have the same energy/fuel/power to propel us forward, or to destroy and damage. Negative emotions can also create a force field of containment, a wall of resistance to action. Negative beliefs and ideas about what you can or cannot accomplish can be "bricks" in your wall of comfort. Your faith-viewpoint gear and emotion gear are both requisites to a strong motivation to action.

RESISTANCE

The Resistor

The zigzag symbol above represents resistance. In the world of electronics, a resistor creates a voltage drop. A dimmer switch in your bedroom is nothing more than a varying resistor. As you turn or slide the control, the lights go dimmer, because the voltage is being reduced or "choked off" between the source and the lamp.

Resistance works the same way in humans, and resistance can take many mental-emotional forms, as shown below. Resistance creates a "voltage" (energy) drop that can slow us down or weaken a person's resilience and drive. We all have resistance in our lives, negative emotions that choke off our energy flow and can "dim our lights."

When electrical current runs through the resistor, it *generates heat* that dissipates into the air. This is what happens to us when we are generating our negative emotional energy into resistance; it dissipates lost energy in the form of heat. And if the current runs too high, it shorts out or blows open, like a fuse causing the circuit to stop functioning.

- FEAR
- LIMITING BELIEF
- LOW CONFIDENCE
- ANGER
- JEALOUSY
- NEGLECT
- UNTRUTH
- MISUNDERSTANDING

Forms of Resistance

Distress, suspicion and uneasiness are all bricks in the wall of resistance that keep us "self-contained" in our comfort zones. When the bricks of guilt, hurt feelings, low self-image, and unbelief stack up enough without resolve, then apathy sets in. And who wants to go back to get more of those feelings and experience the pain of it all again? Ironically, we do need some resistance to gain traction to move ahead, just as airplanes rely on air resistance to gain lift. But in the mental-emotional context we're talking about here, too much resistance can block our forward movement. There is a two-sided coin you will see coming up that is labeled *Hope of Gain* on one side and on the other side, *Fear of Loss*, and it represents the great motivator in us all. We all want to avoid the pain of loss: loss of happiness, enjoyment, and fulfillment.

Bricks of Fear-Based Resistance and Barriers, Gaps, & Diversions

All energy can be altered to be useful instead of destructive or wasted. That means that all of our energy-laden emotions can be rerouted to our benefit. For example, haven't you been able to run your fastest when filled with fear? The energy in the emotion of anger can be converted into the "vow-power" of saying, "I'm never going to let this happen again!" or, "I'm mad as hell, and I'm not going to take it anymore!" This is how unions get started and charities get launched. Anger and contempt go to the root of many human problems if not quickly converted to

232

something good and useful, something that benefits others beyond just yourself. The energy in anger can be converted in order to change your present status and condition if it motivates you to improve and make positive changes. It turns the 5th Gear forward instead of backward. If our self–image is healthy, then the motivation to get out of negative emotional states becomes a driving force to take action and move forward.

Eleanor Roosevelt once said, "You must do the thing you think you cannot do,"[49] which is another way of saying, "feel the fear and move on it anyway." As we saw in the previous chapter on Gear 4, having the right perspective and viewpoint is essential in getting and keeping your hands on the steering wheel of control, your foot on the gas, and your foot off the brake.

The bottom line here is that you can covert negative emotions into push power to make the changes you know you want and need to make, while using your positive emotions as pull power to draw you forward. Faith and love are the strongest emotions and can have the most pulling power. Think what you could do when your pluses and minuses are working as a tag team to accelerate forward progress to your goals. Like a railroad handcar or pump trolley, *every* movement—up or down—would still move you forward. For those of you who don't know what a railroad handcar is, look it up on YouTube. This is how electric motors function with the cycle of positive and negative poles of repulsion and attraction. It's the "motor" mentioned earlier in the Tom Hopkins quote.

When all the previous gears are in good running order, as they should be by now, this business of getting back into the growth zone should come more easily. Remember what we said about empowering framed questions? For example, when you apply your perspective-shaping tool of asking questions like, "What *is* working?," "What's *not* working?," or "What *could* I do right now to change direction?," you will get answers that you can rebuild on in order to put some tread on your tires and get the traction you need to get out of any rut or mud! Coming up in the next chapter, you will be given more tools to ramp up your ability to get into the *growth zone* instead of avoiding it.

Negative feelings can cause you to fall into the gap, trench, or rut and grind your progress to a halt

Emotions Are Signal Generators

"Never apologize for showing feeling. When you do, you apologize for the truth."

-Benjamin Disraeli

Your emotions are the signal generator and transmitter, always putting out a signal frequency, like a two-way radio walkie-talkie. Your emotion-transmitting radio is **always on a channel** or frequency that can be picked up, sent, and received by other people. Have you ever walked into a room or been in an interview (on either side) and had a sense, a vibe or feeling, about the person or group of people? This is where your GPS receives the signal, better described as your EGS (Emotional Guidance Signal), that we described in Gear 1.

Again, emotions don't have to be positive to be useful. Negative emotions have power too. Negative emotions can be *bounced* in a positive direction, like a tennis ball coming at you. You position yourself to step out of its direct path so it doesn't hit you, then you can use that power and energy to move and motivate you forward. It's much wiser to cultivate and leverage your positive emotions, though, because like attracts like and snowballs into a motivating force.

Strong emotions and feelings send signals in two directions: radiating *out* into what Thomas Edison referred to as the "ether," or *into* the subconscious mind, which is where habits are formed and belief systems reside. Emotional energy is magnetic in nature—like a magnet, it has positive and negative poles. If we draw to us what we emotionally focus on, then shouldn't we be very selective about where we "point" our focus? It's been said that **energy** is in motion as **e-*motion,*** and it moves. There are times when a person just can't be positive no matter how hard they try. When this happens, the next best thing is to strive for neutrality. A temporary neutral state is not damaging; it just doesn't move you forward or backward. There are times when a neutral emotion can serve you as a time out, and it can be useful when dealing with intense, over-the-top feelings in either direction. The farther you can step away, the better. Imagine yourself taken up in a hot air balloon 1,000 feet above your emotional incident. The mental act of distancing yourself should create a feeling of much less intensity. The next time you find yourself in a heated argument, for example, try the hot air balloon technique. Not to be confused with apathy or disdain, this could be seen as staying cool with poise under pressure, which is a good leadership quality.

The Transceiver

In the radio communications world, two-way radios are also called transceivers because they are both transmitters AND receivers. Our internal emotional transmitter-receiver is always on when we are consciously awake. Feelings and emotions transmit with or without your awareness; this is referred to as the "principle of radiation." Left to run wild, emotions can create havoc in our lives, drawing to us circumstances and events we may not want or like. Knowing of this interactive power demands that we take control of the emotional "beast" inside us. Like the bit and harness used when riding horses, our feelings and emotions demand *control* and *command*.

Our emotions are signal-generating messengers that tell us whether we are on track or off track from our goals, values, purpose and identity. Like the claxon on ships and submarines, we have built-in yellow and red alert signals. But instead of a signal that sounds like a smoke detector's loud, irritating squeal, it's a signal received by a good or bad feeling. That alarm signal then converts from the mental/emotional realm into a physical feeling in our "gut" or solar plexus, causing increased heart rate, a headache, or muscular tension. Once again, note the interaction between gears: here, our Attention-Awareness Gear works with our Feeling-Emotion Gear. This is an example of **Cogno-Kinetic** energy passing through the gears like the billiard ball example given earlier.

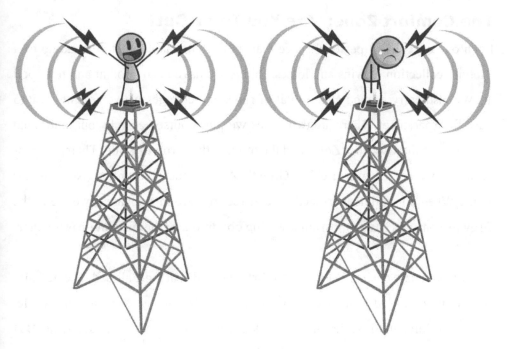

Others can receive your emotional transmitter

As Human Transceivers, We Transmit and Receive Emotional Frequencies

We are all living magnets to what we focus and dwell upon, whether it's negative or positive. Focus is the act of setting the radio channel or frequency. The terms "vibration" and "frequency" are interchangeable. That feeling of being cheated, for example, is an emotion that has power, the power to turn the action gear that says, "I am taking a different path next time." Or better yet, "I'm going to do something right now. I'm going to place that call/write that letter/speak up."

The Comfort Zone: Are You In or Out?

Each one of us has a personal space that feels comfortable, that is made up of a lifetime collection of wins and losses, things we have been good at and not good at. We also carry around a sum total of risks and changes we've assembled into our life experiences. There are two zones we place ourselves in by our emotional state. One is the **Comfort Zone,** and the other is the **Growth Zone.** There is no in-between; we are always in either Growth Zone mode or Comfort (No Growth) Zone. When our beliefs, perspectives and feelings are in resonance, we are in the Growth Zone and have a most empowering condition, a **Cogno-Kinetic** resonance.

One of our basic desires is to get comfortable, and that isn't all bad. We actually need both zones. At times we need rest and comfort to recharge and enjoy life. Some comforts and luxuries that we seek are part of the reason we set goals. **But problems can arise when we dwell in the comfort zone too long,** as addicting as it is. After all, what we really want is "to feel good." When the power and influence of our comfort zone is stronger than our drive to take the risk of going for it, we remain paralyzed. We then lack the drive and momentum to bust through the resistance, the fear wall, or the "terror barrier," as Bob Proctor calls it.[50] Spending too much time in the comfort zone can be deceptive in creating comfort because you can begin to atrophy, much like a leg in a six-month cast gets weaker from lack of activity.

"Go for it!" — "No, don't do it!"

However, the amazing thing about the comfort zone is that as you spend more time in the growth zone, the comfort zone comes right along with you. It's still within arm's reach, but now it has expanded.

Another brick in the barrier wall of false security and comfort that can separate you from advancement is the brick of **indifference** and **laziness.**

"Bricks" of Diversions, Gaps, and Barriers Blocking Growth

These bricks are not always self placed; it's really a combination of both self-placed bricks and "life happens" bricks. Things happen that we did not cause, such as an emergency or an economic event, or a corporate business decision outside our control. Life dictates that <u>there will always be bricks,</u> some of which will never go away. **How we approach and deal with the bricks makes all the difference.** You can position those bricks to form steps that you can climb to a higher station or let them trip you up or block your progress as a wall. Applying the 7 Gears can help you in using the bricks as a road instead of a wall.

The wall of "bricks" represents negative emotions such as unworthiness, apathy, guilt, hurt feelings, anger, resentment, poor self-esteem, and the big one—fear. The common clay in all those growth-blocking bricks is fear, because all of the other feelings stem from fear: fear of what could happen, fear of what won't happen, fear of another failure, and fear of success or criticism. **Other *barrier bricks* can be doubt, worry, apathy, or disbelief.** This is similar to the backpack of rocks you saw earlier, only this time instead of the unnecessary weight of negative "rocks" being carried around, these negative bricks build a confining wall.

"I'll just stay right here where I'm comfy."

- Cog

Fear has two branches. One is actual self-preservation-based fear of something that is real, such as standing on the edge of a cliff or being in harm's way. And then there's the *imagined* fear of some *potential* unpleasant outcome, such as someone laughing at your idea or being rejected when asking someone out on a date. The symbols on the side of each brick represent resistance and blockage. The get-up-and-go charge of positive, empowering energy is shunted by the barriers, gaps, and diversions between where you are and where you want to be. The "bricks" of discouragement, for example, rise to a level that blocks anyone from trying anything new; they just can't be kicked over. Or the bricks of fear, guilt, hurt feelings or sense of unworthiness build a wall of overpowering resistance. Even though we can see Cog sitting there in his cushy chair, the truth is, we are either moving forward or backwards, expanding or contracting, with no real in-between. The life game clock is always running.

Resistance = Noise/Static/Friction

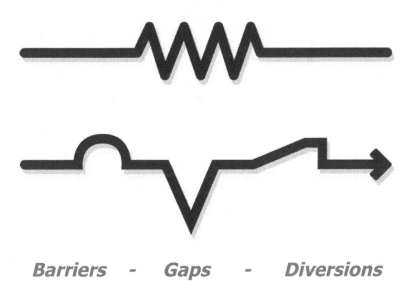

Barriers - Gaps - Diversions

Even though we've all experienced growth zone times, we still can lose sight of how important personal development is if we are ever going to **get off our "can't"** and move forward. If the above Cog graphic were animated, it would show the walls and lines constantly changing because these two zones are always dynamically moving. Both zones are needed to have a balanced, rich, rewarding life and enjoy our accomplishments. We just need to work both sides of the street with balance and make the most of what each zone can do for us in a positive way.

Intense feelings and emotions are much *more powerful* in creating enough drive to take action than positive thinking and self-talk alone. **Intense emotions can overpower our level of conditioning.** Emotion that is intense enough, whether positive or negative, can be like a tsunami that reaches shore, overpowering everything in its path. Examples of intense negative emotion are "crimes of passion" or "temporary insanity." Just as powerful, positive emotional acts of kindness can motivate a person to save someone from drowning with no regard to his or her own safety. **Gear 5 has more push-pull power than all the other gears.**

Deserving or Not Deserving? *You* Decide

Another deceptive resistance barrier to reaching our goals that can push us into the gap is our *self-set* belief level of deserving something. It's deceptive because, like a thermostat, **WE set the level** of deserving our desired outcomes and

245

results. The interaction of **Gears 3, 4, and 5 influence** our mindset of deserving a certain outcome or experience. Recall that we talked earlier about the life-enhancing principle of deep gratitude, its effect on the Law of Increasing Abundance in your life, and how rewarding it can be. Your attitude of sincere, thankful expression rewards you in proportion with what you deserve. This means not just being thankful for the easy, wonderful experiences, but includes the painful failures that result in valuable lessons learned. The more you learn, the more you stand to profit because of the wisdom and maturity you gain from your response to life's ups and downs. Additionally, it's the combined level of **Belief, Viewpoint and Emotion** that set our self-image and confidence level. There are two parts to the emotion of deserving; first, do we **feel** we deserve it, yes or no? And second, at **what level**: *not at all, somewhat*, or *absolutely*? If for any reason you feel you don't deserve something you really long for, then what does that do for your chances of obtaining it? The **feeling** of deserving is sensed at the conscious level, while the controlling **belief** is deeply rooted in the subconscious. Refer to the iceberg graphic a few pages ahead. This explains why we may self-sabotage while striving for a goal, incredible as that sounds. Or we may reach the goal of a certain income level, for instance, but then not be able to hold it. This is why attempting to make changes only at the conscious level can be frustrating because of the strength of our internal programming rules. The feeling of "deserving" something can easily be taken out of context as selfishness or greed, and of course we are not talking about that here. Both wonderful and unpleasant experiences come to us whether we think we deserve it or not. Even so, a healthy amount of the emotion of deserving a positive outcome you earn is one of those hidden ingredients in the self-confidence formula. The feeling of deserving could be called "expecting with a level of certainty." Strangely, the principle of expectations says that whatever you confidently expect or believe you deserve creates a type of self-fulfilling outcome. If we break down the meaning of "according to your faith be it unto you," we see it has multilayered parts. "According to your **Belief (it's possible)** + **Action (I'm doing all I can)** + **Feeling of Deserving** be it unto you." As I'm sure you've experienced, simply feeling you deserve a certain outcome does not guarantee you will receive your desire exactly as you define it. But as the underlying theme of this book suggests, you can influence and alter the probability of realizing your goals and objectives.

"Human behavior flows from three main sources: desire, emotion, and knowledge."

- Plato

A Turn for the Better

We've spent a lot of time on negative emotions and the kinds of damage they can cause. Recognized scientific expert and author Dr. Barbara Fredrickson identifies the **ten most influential positive emotions**: joy, gratitude, serenity, interest, hope, pride, amusement, inspiration, awe, and love. Fredrickson states, "I've learned that these ten forms of positivity color people's day-to-day lives the most."[51] Emotions that have the most empowering energy are worth modeling because of the strength-building charge they infuse you with by delivering harmonious drive to all 7 gears. Instead of creating resistance, these ten emotions cause harmony and maximum positive energy flow. These positive emotions can take the rust off all 7 gears. And they can boost your energy and confidence level to empower you to kick down those bricks of resistance and jettison your backpack of rocks. Then you can escape the comfort zone when you need to and get out into the growth zone, where all future opportunities lie. This list is not all-inclusive, but it brings to light how important positive emotions are in the successful movement of all gears to full running operation.

This next section on Motivation to Action (MTA) should fire you up! This is a big one—the driving force behind making <u>Sustained Unwavering Progress</u> through constant internal motivation!

*The fully empowered running of **Gears 3, 4, and 5** will give you the ability to stay on course and bust through barriers, leap the gaps, and overcome diversions to your success!*

The Combination of Belief, Viewpoint and Emotion Gears blend to form and set YOUR...

Motivation to Action (MTA)

The Key to Constant Internal Motivation

"Some people succeed because they are destined to, but most people succeed because they are determined to."

- Henry Ford

If it doesn't freeze you in your tracks, **fear energy can be a great motivator** to run. As you're about to see, fear of loss is a core motivator: loss of job, loss of relationship, loss of health, loss of security and safety, and of course, loss of life. We are still talking about emotion and the empowering energy it contains. As I mentioned, unchecked anger pointed in the wrong direction can be destructive, but it can also be used as a motivator for positive change. Anger used correctly can put the power in a vow never to be in a certain unpleasant situation again. For instance, you could have a bad experience or witness a major injustice that fires you up enough to demand a change. If you took a trip to Bangladesh or Tijuana, you might see stunning scenes of poverty and deplorable living conditions. And so you launch a program dedicated to fight such atrocities. The energy of all emotions, if channeled properly, can serve us to advance and improve something painful if your perspective-viewpoint (Gear 4) is set right. When you reach a threshold point that says, "That's it! No more of this," that's when motivating action really kicks in, and change happens.

The Propeller is Under the Water

Most of what drives us and propels us forward is **internal,** and much of what blocks our forward motion in barriers, gaps and diversions **isn't consciously visible**. These driving forces can also reside or be launched from the subconscious.

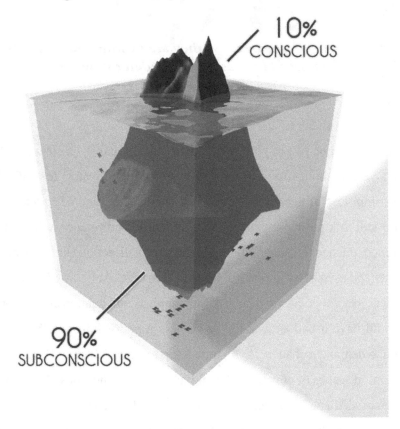

As a sort of servomechanism, the subconscious has multiple functions such as autopilot, cruise control, emotion generator, imagination, and intuition conduit. All incentives come down to those two big motivators, **hope of gain** or **fear of loss**. Like a two-sided coin, both have the *power to push* us and *the power to pull* us one direction or another. Depending on how you use it, it can take you up or take you down.

The Two-Sided "COIN" of Motivation:
The Great Motivator and Source of Drive

There are Two Central Feeling-Based DRIVERS:

1) YOU HAVE TO. For example, you might *have to* stop smoking immediately or lose your life early. You *have to* prepare for the bar exam or you won't get the law degree. You *have to* pay your taxes or go to jail. You *have to* eat to stay alive.

2) YOU WANT TO. For example, either by inspiration, frustration, or intense dissatisfaction, you desire the money, recognition, and reward:

you want to win this year's sales award; you *want to* have a slimmed-down body and the physical feeling of gaining the admiration of others. You *want to* vacation in Bermuda. All of these have their genesis in the two-sided coin stamped **Hope of Gain** and **Fear of Loss**.

As you can see, **Hope of Gain** can be anything that you desire, want or feel you need. **Fear of Loss** is anything that either causes you harm or mental, emotional, or physical pain or discomfort. Notice it's *Fear of...and Hope of...*; meaning it can either be real or *perceived* to be real. Motivation goes back thousands of years for humans. The instinct for survival still comes first. A caveman would hear a roar, and wham! Instant motivation to run! We will soon look at Maslow's Hierarchy of Needs pyramid, where at the base, physiological needs come first.

Both sides of the coin are core motivators; however, research has shown that apathy, laziness, and distractions creep up on us until the big problem gets in our face. Preparing for a test final is often put off until the last day. And sometimes this works, unless it's a math test. You have to be willing to take calculated risks to gain access to the new opportunities waiting for you to be discovered. To take a risk and go for it gets you past the "safe" door and into exciting possibilities.

Fear Is a Great Motivator...in the Opposite Direction

We talked about the energy of fear and its role as a motivator to action **(MTA)**. Fear has great motivating power, meant for our survival against real or perceived danger. It also is the most debilitating feeling known to man because it freezes us up and causes us to stay in our comfort zone—the *NO-GROWTH* zone. Uncontrolled fear  robs us of life by stealing our confidence to act. In its strongest form, it can do the ultimate damage—cut a life short. However, fear is also exciting, and excitement

253

can be a good motivator—if it's kept in perspective. Fear, like dynamite, <u>can be used to damage, but it can also be used constructively</u>. Both uses have an energy and power. The fight-or-flight rush of adrenaline can cause us to perform better, run faster, and be more alert. These are all good things if used from that perspective. Why do we get on a rollercoaster, go through a haunted house, or bungee jump? Because there's an element of excitement in fear, just as there is excitement in feeling hope and realizing that your vacation starts tomorrow or that your new car is ready for delivery. Recall that we said some of your goals should be set with about a 50/50 chance and "scare" you with this same emotion of excitement. Properly channeled fear can serve as an ally instead of an adversary IF the fear is put in *proper perspective* as emotional bricks that can be removed or used as stepping blocks to advancement. Interestingly, **it's the anticipation** of a feel-good or hurtful event that motivates us and not always the reality of what happens.

The "Pilates" of Self-Discipline

Emotional Intelligence

As a kid, every time I heard the term "self-discipline," I had an aversion to it. Maybe it was the "discipline" part that conjured up visions of school. In my grade school at Swanson Elementary, when you were bad or did something wrong, you were banished to sit out in the hallway on the floor, and if the behavior was bad enough, a trip to the principal's office was in order. In junior high, a "bad" kid could be subjected to what they called corporal punishment. Translated- spanking. I never acted up enough in school to get that level of discipline because just the fear factor of the possibility of going to see Mr. Kling was enough to keep me in line. Because of my parents' attempt to drill into me the importance and value of self-discipline, I somehow knew in the back of my mind that it was good for you, kind of like taking cod liver oil or eating wheat germ.

Self-discipline is **a major component** of both **Emotion-Feeling Gear 5** and **Action Gear 7**. You will see how self-discipline plays an important part in successful action. As Jim Rohn says in *Seven Strategies for Wealth and Happiness*, "Discipline is the bridge between thought and accomplishment…the glue that binds inspiration to achievement…the magic that turns financial necessity into the creation of an inspired work of art." Rohn further adds, "Discipline is the foundation on which all success is built. Lack of discipline inevitably leads to failure."[52]

How to Find Out if You Have the "Chutzpah" to Be a Winner

The following proven prescription has the potential to guarantee fabulous, exciting outcomes, giving you the drive to apply all 7 gears. It's a make-or-break test to losing or winning in all eight goal areas of your life. As simple as it sounds, adopting the following power habit could be worth a fortune to you! English Scientist Thomas Huxley put it best when he said,

The most valuable trait that you can acquire is the ability to:
- *make yourself do the thing you should do*
- *when it ought to be done*
- *whether you like it or not.*[53]

What we are really describing here is what has been called the Master Key to success: self-discipline. Self-discipline has been called the Master Key to Success, a key factor in any high achiever, no matter what their field. The right kind of self-discipline is a critical characteristic that makes the difference in succeeding or not. Self-discipline is a kind of force, a component of persistence and perseverance. It means following through to completion, no matter what happens on the barriers, gaps, and diversion path. As mentioned with Gear 6, the power and efficiency of your **Motivation To Action, (MTA)**, or *performance level*, is determined by the alignment and drive coming from all the previous gears. These are some of the key factors in a well-tuned self-discipline machine that ensure you have the emotional intelligence to do what it takes.

1) If you have your Attention-Awareness working well, you are receiving flash ideas through your 6th sense and guidance and feedback through your five senses and your environment.

2) Your **Emotion Gear 5** is generating an energy and signal level of passion that creates the drive to practice, get better, improve, and advance.

3) Your confidence and self-image are on the plus side because **Gears 3, 4, and 5** are tuned to raise your performance level.

4) Your goals, vision images, values, and purpose set in the second gear create the gyroscope and compass that keeps you balanced and on track. Just knowing this is in place can be encouraging and therefore energizing, adding to the push power self-discipline gives you.

Passion Will Push You through Barriers, Gaps, and Diversions

The One Great Motivator That Trumps Them All

All of the Hope-of-Gain or Fear-of-Loss drivers stem from either positive or negative emotions. If someone causes you harm or hurt, for example, you could become *very* motivated by revenge to get even. Other negative emotions like lust, greed, and even hate are proven powerful motivators; history is laced with the devastation and destruction of the outcomes of those who've succumbed to these motivators. But there is one great motivator that trumps them all. It's more powerful than any other type of motivation. And the evidence of its results are strewn throughout human history. I'm sure you've guessed it by now; it's the ultimate supreme power of **love**. Love indeed conquers all. Loving parents know this instinctively. What puts the **Motivation To Action (MTA)** in love? Passion puts the drive in love, which can motivate us to accomplish amazing things. Search any amazing feat in history and you will discover this common denominator. Earlier we covered the motivating power of passion. We've seen in history the power of love driven by passion, such as that of Shah Jahan, who built the famous Taj Mahal driven by love for his wife, Mumtaz Mahal. King Edward VIII gave up his throne for the woman he loved. An entire book could be written about those who have become champions driven by a love and passion for their business: Mother Teresa's passion to help the poorest of the poor, Donald Trump's passion for making deals, Robert Redford and Clint Eastwood's passion for filmmaking. Even more significant than the famous ones are those who are living and expressing their love and passion in daily life, like a single father or mother trying to make ends meet to support his or her children.

The "Self-eSTEAM"-State Generating Machine

In the **Emotion-Feeling Gear 5,** we presented the analogy of how intense desire generates heat, like steam caused by fire underneath a boiler tank. This intense desire ultimately turns the Action Gear. When the Motive To Act **(MTA)** is connected to a strong enough purpose, tremendous pulling or pushing power is released. If you HAD to raise $15,000 in 72 hours in order to save your child's life, could you do it? You bet you would rally up every resource with the highest level of desire and energy power to get it done, to make it happen! We've heard of amazing stories of Herculean feats of strength in a moment of crisis: a woman lifts a car off her son to save him, or a Sherpa mountain guide is able to get a group of climbers up and down Mt. Everest. What's really happening in these instances? The mind-body connection powered by *intense emotion* in a moment rallies all resources to accomplish a goal from places we didn't know existed.

The "I Want It Now" Generation

Each successive generation, it seems, gets more caught up in the powerful pull of **instant gratification.** People demand "instant this" and "instant that." Product and service companies know this and shape their ad campaigns accordingly. We want instant dinners, instant mail, instant banking, and on and on. We get the loan now and figure out how to pay later. I have to work on this challenge myself because there are times when the temptation to "get it now" is just too great.

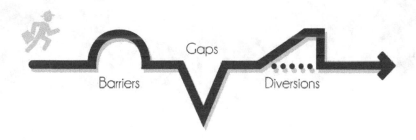

You will see once again the graphic above referencing barriers, gaps, and diversions. Throughout the book, these depictions represent mostly self-imposed limitations.

Fear and Doubt Can Knock Cogs off Your Gears

When any of the 7 gears are not moving smoothly forward, it may stem from a damaged gear that's missing teeth, such as a bad attitude, a disempowering belief system, a lack of awareness or action, ignorance about an important fact or truth, or simply one bad decision.

Gears missing some teeth from neglect form a weak, ineffective system

Interestingly, barriers, gaps, and deviations contain an important common denominator in success. With clear direction and enough persistence, you get through to the other side and you pick up an energy force. You're stronger and a bit wiser because of the experience and can use the wisdom gained for future events.

If you could interview the movers and shakers and industry leaders, athletes, recording artists, movie stars, and top medical doctors and nurses, you would find one common theme or pattern. They're all passionate about their jobs; they all put in the hard work. Actress Julie Andrews advises, "Sometimes opportunities float right past your nose. Work hard, apply yourself, and be ready. When an opportunity comes, you can grab it."[54] If you're really on fire with positive emotion about what you do, then the idea of discipline won't scare you off. Haven't you ever had a time when you got so into an event or activity that time flew by? And if there was work, it didn't *feel* like work at all?

As complex and diverse as we all are, **different motivators** may drive one person more effectively than someone else. All are purpose-driven values according to our hierarchy of values or what we consider important. In the work arena, money is most often a factor, but money alone may not be the complete driving force. Most people define personal fulfillment as loving what you do, making a contribution, and being a part of something big and exciting. For me, that was a big motivator.

Worry vs. Concern

It's not possible to always avoid worry because it's a part of our makeup. Worry is a **first cousin to fear**, and when out of control, switches from serving us as an alert to paralyzing us. For those who would say, "Being worried shows I'm concerned," know that there is a difference. Unchecked worry can become a self-centered, endless loop of attention only on the problem, but concern has a proper sensitivity to a problem or issue. Concern is a more open-ended feeling that quickly focuses on alternatives working toward a solution. Treat worries like tennis balls and smack them away from you. You acknowledge the emotion coming at you, but quickly send the worry ball to the solution side of the court.

What Determines What We All Really Want?

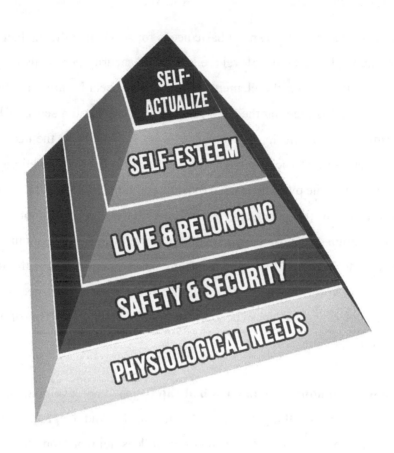

Abraham Maslow's Hierarchy of Needs

Maslow's Hierarchy of Needs

For as long as records have been kept, humanity has had an inborn drive and curiosity to reach for more, to explore, expand, improve, and grow. In 1943, psychologist Abraham Maslow created a list of our top desires, motivations, and needs by priority. Presented here as a pyramid, his hierarchy suggests that people are motivated first to fulfill basic, essential life needs before moving up to the more complex requirements.

The first level addresses the most basic needs for survival at the instinct level: air, water, and food. On the next level are safety and security needs, also important to survival: shelter from the elements, steady work, health care, and safety from danger. Level 3 is meeting the need for love, affection and a sense of belonging, friendship, companionship, and romance. Next, on level 4, is the need for a high level of self-esteem, social recognition, and accomplishing something of value. And at the top of the pyramid is what Maslow calls self-actualization, where people are **self-aware**, fulfilling personal growth and satisfying their full potential. **Desire and motivation are close cousins,** and any form of ambition contains these two elements. Motivation is derived from many sources and contains the reasons for WHY we yearn for the things we want. Maslow's hierarchy of needs hits on the core reasons why one may become motivated. However, we often set our expectations governor on low.

Willpower and hope have taken a bad rap by personal development coaches in recent years as something that just doesn't work. And I agree; depending on willpower alone as a motivator in and of itself does not work long term. Hope and willpower have been misunderstood to be self-sustaining motivators because most people don't get how they fit into the total success formula. Like a pilot light to a furnace, hope and willpower are weak at first but serve as important ignitors to the larger flame of drive and passion. They must be sustained, like an airplane engine, and continue running to stay aloft. Maintaining a high enough level of commitment combined with the three gear factors mentioned earlier creates the empowered STATE you must have to keep you moving forward. If the preceding conditions are in place, hope and willpower can be very effective. Haven't you experienced this yourself at times?

Comfort Zone: Wall of Safety or Growth Barrier?

"The comfort zone is a major obstacle to ambition, desire, determination, and accomplishment."[55]

- Brian Tracy

As mentioned earlier, spending some time in the comfort zone is needed; yet by dwelling there too long, it can be a cage that traps you from making further progress. Sustained unwavering discomfort outside the comfort zone for too long can also be disempowering. We should be thankful for the comforts we've earned or been given, but we must balance the comfort zone with kicking down or climbing up and over the brick wall of resistance and spend more time in the growth zone. It's not one or the other; it's balancing both. In the next chapter we'll explore what's so great about getting into the growth zone.

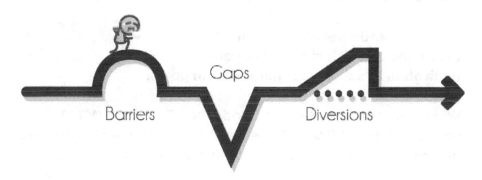

How do you take down the wall of resistance, leap over the gap, or plow through diversions? **When the three GEARS of Belief/Viewpoint/Feeling blend together, they create what is called STATE or MINDSET or being IN THE ZONE!** When these three gears are turning smoothly in the right direction, you will have enough power and drive to bust through any barriers, gaps or diversions that come at you!

<u>Worth Remembering</u>

- Whenever you hear the phrase "mindset," think of the three gear-factors, Faith-*Belief/Perspective-Viewpoint/Emotion-Feeling,* that make a mindset-state.

- Your emotions are *not* out of your control.

- You're never defeated *until* you stop trying.

- Your self-set self-image sets the boundaries of your performance level.

- The depth and level of your desires determines the steam power of your motivation to act on your purpose and goals.

- When it comes to motivation, Motivation To Action (MTA), intense white-hot Desire leaps past any motivational technique, perceived negative limitations, or any preset conditioning.

- Love trumps all motivating factors because love contains passion and zeal that delivers enough power to climb the mountain or move the mountain!

- The "master key" to success is building the type of consistent *internal* motivation that keeps Sustained Unwavering Progress and Daily Action Habits (SUPDAH) moving you ahead in spite of any barriers, gaps or diversions.

- Just as your IQ is not locked, your EQ (Emotional Quotient) is not set either. You can direct it into forward-moving drive.

- Remember that what really matters is not the event or experience, but HOW you FEEL about the event!

- Summary: When your level and polarity of <u>Feelings-Emotions</u> change, your outcomes and conditions change.

Worth Doing

- When caught up in the past or in fears about the future, make a habit in the moment to get back to your *tangent now* point, or use your new "Daily Dozen."

- Because fear is also a *state of mind*, apply everything you've learned to control it with the "bit and bridle" of material in this book and put it in its place.

- Practice assembling one good feeling onto another, building more today than yesterday. Make it fun!

- Continually update your "Daily Dozen" good feeling reference list and keep it at arm's length, e.g., on your smartphone, in your purse or wallet.

- Always strive to make anyone you encounter feel better because of something you say or do!

- We all get angry at times; that's not a problem when you treat those moments like an Emotional Aikido master: just step aside and let the *energy of the reason you're angry* swish past you.

- When someone is directing their anger at you, be an Emotional Aikido master and step aside from the "kick" coming at you.

- You are always in charge of your happiness. So what are you doing about it, boss?

- Practice putting good feelings *ahead* of the happy event! This is much more powerful than you think!

Your Motivation To Action

influences your...

STATE OF MIND-CONFIDENCE:

The Growth Zone

"A man changes the state of his outer world by first changing the state of his inner world."[56]

- U.S. Anderson

The Secret Alloy

What Is It Made Of?

The last chapter centered on the comfort zone and the problems that go with it. In this chapter, we're going to focus on the **growth zone** area. In the book *The*

Achievement Zone, Shane Murphy describes the zone as what athletes recognize as "a special place where their performance is exceptional and consistent, automatic and flowing."[57] Murphy reveals that Olympic-level athletes invest about as much time in honing their *internal mindset* as they do training their bodies. We must duplicate that same ratio to make certain our goals are reached and our results and outcomes are fantastic.

Motivation is the primary key to ambition. As we touched on in earlier chapters, the energy of desire and motivation are close cousins. Why is it that some appear ambitious, while others are satisfied to coast through life and just see what happens? Any thirst for achievement cannot be found in one's DNA or surroundings because ambition is an attitude of mind, a *state of mind* that is composed primarily of the full running of Gears 3, 4 and 5. The turning of those gears as a collective form of ambition or drive can be induced from any number of sources, such as the intense desire for financial freedom, a sense of duty to act responsibly, serving others, or leading a cause that you are passionate about, to name but a few. Not all motivations are of good cause, though; consider the intense greed for power over others, an overwhelming desire for revenge, or jealousy to sabotage someone's good fortune or honest work. In any case, the common denominator still includes a burning desire for some area of achievement. Remember how we said that the weak desire of hope is like a pilot light to a bigger flame? When desire is reinforced by the highest form of belief (the flame of conviction), your outcomes and results are more likely to meet with certainty. Let's recall the four-part belief system identified in **Gear 3, Faith-Belief;** the miracle-making conduit that generates a level of certainty that can move mountains. They are: ***Faith in Yourself*** (Confidence), ***Faith and Belief in a Higher Power, Faith and Belief in an Opportunity***, and ***Faith and Belief in a favorable Outcome,***

271

Result, or Condition. Once again, your level and range of confidence sets your internal state of mind, your "engine order telegraph" (the speed that the bridge orders to the engine room on a ship or submarine). It's what puts the pedal to the metal on your performance setting.

It's "Why" Power That Feeds Willpower

Another part of our internal performance machine is the mental-emotional force of willpower. *BUT* in order to be a force, it must be fortified by all the previous gears to get us through to worthwhile accomplishment. When willpower is *intense* and *sustained* with a white heat fire of desire to complete the task or reach the goal, you'll have the level of drive needed to feed and maintain persistence. And that fire of desire always comes from REASONS—WHY you're taking action.

The power of knowing why we do something can be a huge motivator, even to the point of temporarily overriding internal programming and conditioning—in the moment. For example, if you had a fear of water that stemmed all the way back to your childhood, you could temporarily override that deep-rooted fear if you saw someone drowning and calling for help. In that moment, you could jump in the water and get the person to safety. Later, coming to your "senses," you might think, "Hey, how did I do that?" The **reason** to act overpowered any previous mental or emotional conditioning. Big enough reasons put juice in your willpower and speed up your drive to act sooner rather than later.

Perform-O-Stat

There's been a lot of discussion in self-development circles about how our performance level is like a house thermostat. Let's say you have an internal program that says, "I can sell $100,000 worth of business in a year; that's all," but then you sell over $150,000 the next year. Somehow, in some way, you sabotage yourself to drop back down the next year to $100,000 in business sold. This is how a thermostat works: you set it for 70 degrees in the room, and if the room temperature drops below 70, the furnace kicks in.

When the room goes above 70 degrees, the thermostat kicks in again, only this time it shuts the furnace off so the temperature can drop back down to 70. I've coined the term **"Perform-O-Stat"** as a more accurate way of describing human performance levels. The *Perform-O-Stat* symbolizes the measurement and reading of our physical and mental-emotional levels in the moment. Like a thermostat, it also identifies our desired set point of performance and how close we are to the actual required outward level of execution. It could also be called *"Perform-O-State"* because everything we're describing here has to do with the blended triad, the mental-emotional-physical state we are in at any given moment and how that directly affects our performances. As we've all experienced, *the state you're in* affects the quality and caliber of your decisions and choices, Gear 4. Further, it influences how you respond to an event or experience. At this point in the book, I hope you can see how all of these gears are interrelated, interactive, and interdependent as factors that influence the quality of our outcomes, results, and conditions!

You Set Your Perform-O-Stat by
Gears 3, 4, & 5

The Perform-O-Stat

Who sets and adjusts the controls of your Perform-O-Stat? You do! Never forget that because when you drop your Attention-Awareness, Gear 1, of this critical fact, then you will fall back into the default cork-on-the-water drift mode by which the majority of people live. I believe you know too much now to let that happen ever again!

Sadly, most people's **Perform-O-Stats** are rarely set to allow full potential through. *They run with their self-imposed governor on.* Lawnmowers and go-karts have what's called a governor to set the limits of the engine performance, usually at about one-third of its full capacity. It's sad because many people just aren't aware of their built-in gift of a Perform-O-Stat or don't get how important it is in gaining mastery and control over their outcomes and results.

State Baseline

Neuro-Linguistic Programming (NLP) practitioners believe we all have a "state-baseline," a state that we feel most comfortable in. I believe this baseline state has a lot to do with our comfort zone. Authors Joseph O'Connor and Ian McDermott tell us in their book, *Principles of NLP*, that we should consider our baseline state from four different viewpoints:

1. "Your physiology: the state of your body." In other words, health and energy level.
2. "Your thoughts: your level of attention, awareness and mental energy...mental pictures." Hey, that's Gear 1!
3. "Your predominant emotion. Is it happy, sad, angry?"
4. "Your spiritual state. How you relate to something larger than yourself."

O'Connor and McDermott add that "we take our beliefs and values, behavior and capabilities from our parents, and we often take the state that goes with them."[58]

When it comes to the mindset of being in the zone, *we can't be "up" all the time, but we can do certain things* that will tip the scale of positive states to outweigh a negative condition. Having a positive **State of Mind,** or confidence level, in "**The Zone**" (or "the groove," or whatever you label it) is almost always created out of a blended combination of **three Gears:** *Faith-Belief + Perspective-Viewpoint + Feeling-Emotion*. It's this combination of gears that is the **supercharger** to the next two Gears ahead: **Decision and Action.** The combination also leads ultimately to successful outcomes, results, goals, or realized experiences.

Cage or Catapult?

To be in **the Zone** is what all champions in all fields seek. Olympians and all athletes are after this mindset of aligned empowerment because they know it's the winning edge requirement, the difference that makes the difference. The difference between first and second place, between gold and bronze medals, is often measured in milliseconds, centimeters, or grams. Is it all just luck or timing alone? Or is there something more to it?

As an expert in sports psychology, Dr. Gayle A. Davis has worked with every type and level of athlete, including Olympic figure skaters. After 20 years in sports psychology, Davis discovered that the techniques and principles that improved all levels of sports performance could be applied to other life areas. In her book *High Performance Thinking,* Davis says, "By consistently combining mental skills with physical skills, anyone can improve their performance, whether that performance is at a board meeting or on the playing field, at the PTA or the PGA."[59] Davis describes working with figure skaters, practicing over 1,000 hours a year for just 20 minutes total of competition. She says that although massive effort has been invested in technical skills and nutrition for energy and endurance, a skater's mental skills and self-confidence may be weak. Davis adds, "She needs to know that the greatest resource that any athlete brings to competition is their mind" and that "some experts say that as much as 95% of our performance is mental after we have skill development."[60]

Self-confidence, a key to attainment, is one of our most wanted and needed traits. It overrides fear, doubt, and insecurity and is a byproduct of Gears 3, 4, and 5. Those with high levels of confidence are the leaders, the movers and shakers in our society, even if only in the arena that they are passionate about. Everyone has a high confidence level in *some* area of their lives; it could be tennis, sales, carpentry, sewing, or organizing events. Our self-confidence level is that same combination of **attitude, belief**, and **feeling;** hence the term "**state**." It is not an ability or skill. You can't borrow it or buy it because it comes from within. It is an internal feeling—intangible, invisible—and yet you must feel it. So-called champions in the arts, sciences, athletics, and business pass through the lower levels first, a sort of "rite of passage" transitioning from one level to the next.

"MOTOR"-Vation

In the automotive world of drag racing, car engine technicians will install superchargers on top of the engine to "ram" air into the intake and boost engine performance. In the same way, your internal STATE "engine" gains power through the turbo-charging booster of the three gears: **Faith with Certainty, Can-Do Attitude, and "Let's do this!" Feeling.** Running in sync, they supercharge your **confidence and self-esteem** and sharpen your focus on the task at hand. This then drives the **Motivation to Action (MTA)** into rocket-sled power. Additionally, when **Gear 2,** your **Operating System-Blueprint,** is sharp, compelling, and clear, you have the winning combination pointing in the right direction, screaming you past the checkered flag!

Are you running a hamster cage motor OR...

A high-performance supercharged engine?

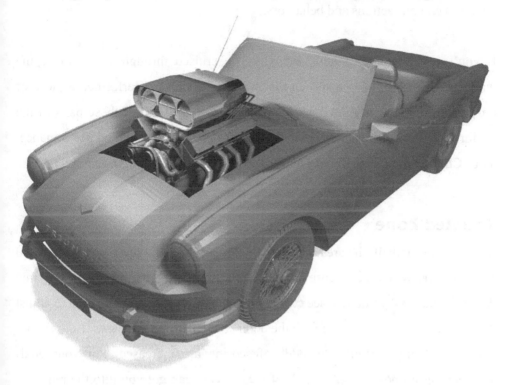

Your three-gear combo state determines your
horsepower

You Need N₂O to Make It Go!

Another power-boosting technique in high performance dragsters is NOS, a **Nitrous Oxide System.** This system boosts engine power even more by creating additional oxygen in the cylinders. Sometimes your "octane" level of hoping and wishing is too low to fire the engine and take off. Only high performance fuel, the "nitrous-oxide" mixture of *strong belief, optimism, intense positive emotion* and *full-out commitment* will send you forward at the rate and velocity you need. Your state of mind is either the *governor* (limiting your speed) or the *supercharger* (hit the gas!) on your actions and behaviors.

If you've ever wondered how and why you cruised through a test, made the winning jump shot, gave a speech that was well received, performed a piece of music flawlessly, or mastered a winning deal, this is it! All of these parts of the Perform-O-Stat is the primary *combo-cause* that created the winning performance. Your **Confidence Level Belief Gear+ Attitude Gear+ Feeling Gear = STATE.**

The Red Zone

In American football, the area between the 20-yard line and the goal line is called the **red zone**. When the offense is in that area, strategies change, and so does the defense. That's why you will see coaches and quarterbacks call a time out to adjust their strategy. The intensity of both the defense and offense increases. Both teams' strategies change because the odds of scoring are increased. For your goal-achievement purposes, applying all of these Gears can get you into the red zone more often.

Make Steel

As I mentioned in the introduction, one of the synergistic benefits of the seven gears is how they are **combined and arranged**, a difference that can make *all* the difference in getting what you want. To make steel, for example, you must have a mixture of iron, carbon, manganese, and chromium. To have the strong "sword" of an empowered state, you need the combination of belief, right viewpoint, and positive emotion. These metaphors should drive home the importance of the best use of all the Gears, especially **Gears 3, 4, and 5** in creating confidence, a stronger self-image, and a raised **Perform-O-Stat**. An amalgamation of the right materials or factors makes a stronger product than the individual elements. The same principle applies to the combining factors of **Belief** + **Perspective** + **Intense Feeling.**

The Magnetic Force

One of the side benefits of being in an empowered state is that it produces an **electrical charge** of sorts that creates a contagious magnetic influence: enthusiasm. It radiates that "certain something" that others are drawn to. Some would call it charisma, or star power. This is the state all athletes and world-class performers seek, whether it's in the board room, on the set, or on the stage.

This magnetic force can work both ways, positive and negative. For example, being around a negative person can have the same magnetic influence on you. If your self-image and state is strong, a negativity-radiating person will repel you, but if your overall state is down and weak, then you will be pulled into the negative influence. Hence the cliché "misery loves company."

Self-Image: A Performance Regulator

In his monumental 1960 book *Psycho-Cybernetics*, plastic surgeon Maxwell Maltz discovered a mysterious connection between a patient's psychology and their facial improvement surgeries. In particular, he observed the powerful effects of people's self-image. In many cases he reported that his scalpel "became a magic wand" in transforming patients' physical looks. Some personalities changed for the better, while others did not. The *great discovery* was that in all his case histories, the self-image was the determining factor.[61] The amazing self-proclaimed power of self-image is a prerequisite to self-esteem and self-confidence and, therefore, your "ability" to perform at a certain level, the **Perform-O-Stat.**

Confidence + Self-Image + Self-Esteem + STATE =
Your performance level

When you go to work on the elements of the Perform-O-Stat in the model above, you build the supercharger in your engine, the key to gaining traction and mastery over your outcomes, results and goal experiences!

The COMBINATION OF Belief, Viewpoint and Emotion Gears blend to form and set your...

PERFORM-O-STAT

Your level and number of accomplishments are determined by the setting of your **Perform-O-Stat**. *You* set the level, no one else.

Inner Game—Outer Game:

What's Running in Your Inner Mind Affects Your Outer World

"We build too many walls and not enough bridges."

- Isaac Newton

Cog realizes that in order to advance and grow, he needs to get out of the comfort zone!

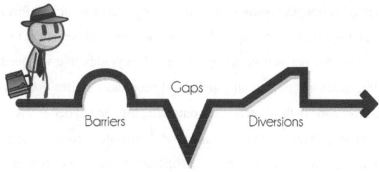

Barriers and gaps will never completely go away; because life happens, they will always be there. And they are no respecter of persons. The rain falls on the just and the unjust.[62] The "jungle" is what it is.

I like how Author Steve Chandler puts it in his book *100 Ways to Motivate Yourself,* where he talks about running head on into your fear barriers: "The world's best-kept secret is that on the other side of your fear, there is something safe and beneficial waiting for you." He also says "if you pass through even a thin curtain of fear, you will increase the confidence you have in your ability to create your life."[63]

These adversities, roadblocks and obstacles have a benefit IF our state is high and our awareness is keen to any possible benefit, as paradoxical as that sounds. The *benefit* is like that of going to a gym to work out and lift weights. The strain of the workout creates a benefit of increased strength and vitality when you return for the next workout. Passing through any of life's barriers or obstacles creates *a new level of character and wisdom* that, with the right perspective, can better empower us for the inevitable next round of challenges. When you overcome *any* size of obstacle, there's always a lesson learned or a new bit of wisdom that can be added to your arsenal for the next encounter.

In Brian Tracy's book *Maximum Achievement,* he describes our comfort zone as a "homeostatic impulse." Tracy says, "It is your unconscious tendency to be drawn irresistibly toward what you've always done." Tracy adds that we need to keep aware of this mechanism, "but all growth and progress requires you to move out of your comfort zone in the direction of something bigger and better." And perhaps most importantly, "You must consciously and deliberately counter the pull of the comfort zone as you move upward and onward toward ever-higher levels of accomplishment."[64] And that is what these 7 Gears are about: building you into a whole new-and-improved person with an upgraded Gear 2 Operating System that can use Cause and Effect instead of having Cause and Effect use you. Your confidence and self-efficacy clicks up a notch, making you better prepared for higher challenges and the rewards that come with the price of personal development.

Just as we have a different self-image for different things, we have more than one mindset. There is a mindset toward wealth, a mindset towards health, and one for each of the eight goal areas including Relational, Career, Family, Home, Recreation, Mental, and Spiritual. So a mindset is really a collection of beliefs, attitudes, and emotions that mix and meld together. The ingredients of concrete or a cake by themselves have some value, but with the **RIGHT combination?** Bingo! The safe door is open to the valuable riches and rewards inside.

As was mentioned earlier, we operate on varying channels on different frequencies. Neuroscience experts have discovered that what is often referred to as "state" or **"mindset"** is a level of readiness that is actually a combination of biochemistry and aligned brainwave patterns. We've all experienced the calming effects of certain music and nature sounds such as hearing ocean waves, wind through the trees, or mountain streams. Certain sounds or music can be added to your tools for empowering state change. Haven't you heard a song that takes you back to a specific time in your life and causes you to relive where you were, what you were doing, or even what you were feeling in that moment? In that moment, you were transported to that state. This is powerful, and you should use tunes that give you an empowering feeling. Recall the "Daily Dozen" technique from Gear 4. It's been reported that actor Johnny Depp plays music during his acting scenes to boost his performance. Why does the military have theme songs? To boost troops' emotions into an empowering state.

There are methods of altering mental focus and consciousness available for your arsenal of state-changing tools without the need for drugs or alcohol. Much research has been conducted on the science of peak performance and what internal conditions exist when one is in the ideal mental-emotional state of intense focus, often called "flow" by experts on the subject.[65] Check out the music of Mozart; some of his pieces have been proven to sharpen one's focus state. In particular, neuroscience researchers have determined that Mozart's K448 Sonata for Two Pianos in D Major influences concentration.[66]

Recall the six higher faculties of the human mind in the Gear 1 chapter. We explored how weak willpower is as a sole source motivator. And the reason for this is that willpower functions mostly in the conscious mind, while the subconscious contains the entrenched attitudes, emotions, and habits. Now that you have Gears 3, 4, and 5 running at peak performance, your decisions and choices (Gear 6) will be quicker, smarter, and more effective. Now you have REAL willpower, willpower that is beefed up enough to *sustain* you to your goals and aspirations. The outcome-causing factor of an ***empowered state*** has the potential to create life quality improvements beyond what you've experienced so far.

Cog got through the wall and out into
the Growth Zone!

"*Unless you try to do something beyond what you've already mastered, you will never grow.*"

- Ralph Waldo Emerson

Worth Remembering

- Your mindset is an important driver to your momentum and habits.

- Your success depends on the support and cooperation of other people AND your application of all 7 gears—it's the one-two punch.

- While your success depends on the support of other people, don't fasten your happiness to a thing or person.

- The Emotion of Love/Passion/Desire—Gear 5—has caused all progress in history and is _the_ motivating factor to your Motivation.

- "Inch by inch, anything's a cinch," means baby steps are doable and keep you moving forward.

- Mindsets, like any fine-tuned motor, require regular tune-ups and inspections.

- Logic almost always rides shotgun, while emotion is in the driver's seat.

- "Where there's a will, there's a way" really means, "where there's a _big enough reason,_ there's a way."

- Work magically changes into a fun ride when you combine your mindset with the first five Gears.

- Summary: When your <u>State of Mind and Motivation to Action</u> change, your outcomes, results and conditions change.

Worth Doing

- Inspect your mindset by examining your faith, perspective, and emotion gears for "rocks" in your backpack—disempowering erroneous beliefs from an earlier time.

- Create your own custom state-changing music list.

- Right now, start assembling your list of REASONS for going after your goals and outcomes, and watch your MTA (Motivation to Act) blast off! Your number of emotion-laden reasons determines your number of booster rockets! (This is one of the crown jewels of MTA!)

- Drill into your mindset that your *little micro-successes* add up and snowball into bigger successes.

- Refer to your "Daily Dozen" for state-enhancing remembrances you assembled.

- You have been gifted with talents that can send you soaring. Go back to your 1st/2nd gears if you don't have a clear idea of what your best talents and abilities are.

Your State of Mind powers and influences your...

Gear • 6

DECISION-CHOICE

"You are not born a winner.
You are not born a loser.
You are born a chooser. "

- Anonymous

Internal Action

When you make a **choice or a decision,** you are have already taken your *first* action, an **internal action**. You now have a "yes" or "no" about the direction you're headed. It may not be in the physical realm yet, but it's just as real. It's the first ignition point; you've just thrown the ignition switch on the launch pad!

When you think about it, our daily waking activities are a <u>continuous, unending chain of decisions and choices.</u> Researchers have determined that the average adult human makes thousands of conscious decisions each day. And every single daily decision is influenced and biased by all five previous connecting gears. Always- at some level. These hidden unconscious influencers are dynamic and ever changing in their intensity and priority.

This means that these ever-changing conditions may cause you to make a different decision about the same thing ten minutes later! It's a lot like driving in traffic. The arrangement of cars and trucks *in the moment*, combined with changing speeds, traffic lights, road conditions and lane changers in front of you demand quick decisions. A fire truck comes up behind you. A dog darts out in front of you. The traffic light turns yellow; are you going run through it or slow down and stop? Someone ahead of you hits their brakes. In order to make it safely to your destination, you must make several instantaneous decisions based on a multitude of influences and conditions. This is just a sample of how never-ending changing variables affect our decisions.

So Many Decisions, So Many Choices!

Consider how your choices have piled up to take you in a certain direction and have influenced your destiny. Think about how the sum of all your choices up to this point has put you exactly where you are, whether good or bad, happy or unhappy. Two sons are raised in the same family, but Dave runs for Congress, while his brother is in prison. Both destinies are the summation of small daily decisions and not entirely the result of environment.

It's not always the big decisions that determine our outcomes and shape our destiny. Moment-to-moment decisions add up at the end of the day, assembling an invisible collection of choices that build up to either a great future or lousy life experience. What's so easy to forget is how powerful this is in shaping and steering our future! We are always making the choices. Always! Even if you say, "Well, I just won't decide; I'll leave that up to someone else," **you still made a decision.** This is of such importance that it warrants rereading this paragraph!

We are constantly weighing pros and cons of every choice and decision: "I will do this! I won't do that!"

Pros and cons are biased by our Comfort Zone and the emotions that guard it! And those mini evaluations stack up at different rates (from seconds to weeks, months, or years) and at different mental-emotional depths (consciously, semiconsciously, or unconsciously). We are always weighing self-proclaimed pros and cons as *good/not good* or *like/don't like,* tipping the scale of every decision. Many, if not most, of our decisions are tied into our comfort zone, something we learned about in the last chapter. And our comfort zone or un-comfort/growth zones are made up of a dynamic, ever-changing collection of confidence-building or confidence-robbing emotions and feelings. That's why Gear 5 is positioned where it is. Decisions can be influenced all the way back to our Operating System (Gear 2), where values, purpose, and goals reside. When we begin to MOVE on our decisions and choices, then we get the REAL go/no-go pedals! Gear 5 kicks in and says, "Are you really prepared to handle the consequences of this decision and the negative emotions you might encounter?" "What if I fail?" "What if it doesn't work out?" "What if she says no?" Many times we have to decide what we are going to release in exchange for our new decision. We can only have a grip on one decision at a time. For example, if you decide to go to Chicago University next semester, you give up going to the University of Denver. Or if you sit down at your favorite Italian restaurant and choose chicken Alfredo (a.k.a. heart attack on a plate) over minestrone soup (a healthy option), you might eat and then cry, "Oh, why did I do that?" Every decision we make comes with that two-sided coin called risk/opportunity, which you will be learning about just ahead.

In the world of engineering, troubleshooting diagrams include a series of decision points that show up as we try to identify the source of a problem. One of those symbols is the *diamond decision point* you see diagrammed under the 6th Gear. When you come to a decision point you have options, many times more than just one, as represented by the lines in the Cog Choice graphic above. And because our level of awareness is limited, we most likely have more options than we know. Sometimes it is truly just a fork in the road, but other times you may have several options.

Decision Point

> *"Two roads diverged in a wood and I –*
> *I took the one less traveled by,*
> *And that has made all the difference."*

- Robert Frost, *"The Road Not Taken"*

Direction Setter

Smarter, wiser decisions mostly stem from a ***combination*** of choice-making skills learned from practice and other factors called out in the previous gears. Recall the rewards of self-discipline, and in particular the three-step method given by Thomas Huxley: doing what you should do, whether you like it or not, when it needs to be done. Applying these valuable traits puts an end to the debilitating problem of indecision and the price tag of frustration and regret that goes with it later on.

This is where your direction is set, and your decisions point your direction. What you choose points the way to your future and destiny.

Decisions happen in an instant, in the present moment, although some may be preceded by cumulating factors gathered over days, weeks, and even years. Nevertheless, choices and decisions are a ***point of power***. The effects of your immediate decisions can have major results later on. Even if you say, "Well, I simply *won't* decide right now; I'll put it off," in that moment, you just inserted one decision before the next! There is no such thing as "no choice," because "no choice" **is** a choice!

Having all the cogs on the previous five gears, especially Gear 2, will knock out indecision and doubt as well as the anxiety that goes with it.

Let me say it one more time: everything and everyone you encounter matters, and they all add up to influence your collection of daily decisions! A **Decision-Choice** made is the "flint" that sparks the **Action Gear**.

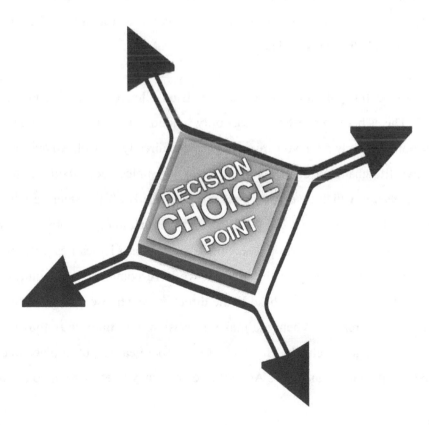

The First Point of Power

All 7 gears have an energy and power level unto themselves, but there are **two places** in the 7 Gears that generate movement: the outward *physical action* you must have to progress, and the internal *act of making a decision*. Making a decision is a **point of power** because this is where you really perform your first act. When you **decide**, you've instantly set the direction. Like a bolt of lightning, it's quick and carries a spark of energy. Maybe you have fretted over a decision and then suddenly said, "This is it; I'm going this way," or, "I'm ready to quit smoking right now." And in that moment didn't you feel like you just took a rock or two out of your backpack? In other words, you felt a little lighter, energized by the simple act of resolve. More often than not, when you make a choice it has a liberating feeling. There's a feeling of release. The word "decide" originally meant "to settle a dispute" or "to cut off." When you decide, there's no retreat; you're moving forward and the dispute is settled.

The two essential **points of power** are **Decision-Choice, Gear 6**, and **Action, Gear 7**. This is because these two gears only function in the present moment—the **NOW** point, the only point you are empowered to directly control. No one can take these two life-changing elements away from you unless you abdicate them to someone else, in which case you are taking your hands off the steering wheel of control. As ludicrous as that sounds, it's a sad fact that many people unwittingly hand over their gift of control to someone else. The past is dead as dirt, and the future isn't here yet. Only in the *now* do we have command and control and, therefore, the power to move ahead in the direction we choose. It's been said that now is the only reality. When you make a decision, you **take your foot off the brake** and engage the clutch. There's just one more gear to put in place and put the pedal to the metal, and that's Action! Are you ready? Let's *decide* to *go for it!*

Our Co-pilot and Creator has gifted us control over our thoughts and choices. In *How To Raise Your Own Salary,* Andrew Carnegie tells Napoleon Hill, "The only thing the individual has to do is to take charge of his own mind and exercise this control. That is something he cannot neglect or avoid without condemning his entire life to the stray winds of chance!"[67] This means *we* must take purposeful command and control over our thinking, including making wise decisions that are referenced to our values, purpose and goals—Gear 2. Yes, we are already making thousands of decisions every day. But to consciously practice your decision making with the express intent of speeding you toward reaching your eight goal areas and your clearly defined life purpose…ahhh! That is the difference that will make *the* difference in living a much more rewarding life. I think you can see now just how important the well-running movement of Gears 1 through 5 are in empowering you with a superior ability to make the best decisions possible. This is the ignition point where the internal six working gears **begin** the journey into reality and start the outward transition of manifesting effects and outcomes.

Making a decision initiates the first stage of commitment. I say **first stage** because you may make a decision, start into that direction, and then change your mind later. There are times when you may realize that your decision was not a good one, and you're better off heading in another direction because of new information or a new condition that tells you, "This way isn't working, or it's wrong!"

Recall that we talked about the **backpack of feelings and beliefs** we carry around when we could be carrying a jet pack like the one James Bond flew in *Thunder Ball* or the new Martin Jetpack. Again, we can decide to jettison those rocks, set the backpack down, and walk away from it!

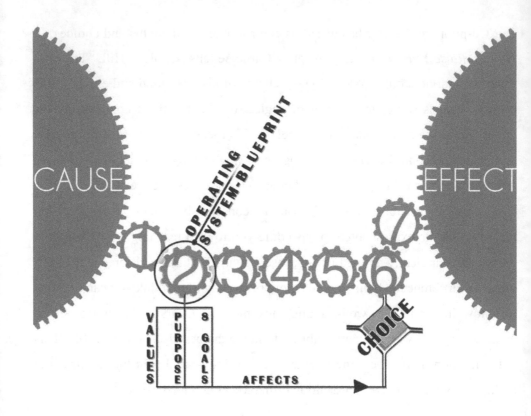

Gear 2 has a direct and powerful effect on Gear 6, your decisions

While it's true that the **6th Gear** of **Decision-Choice** is positioned between Gears 5 and 7, it is *Cogno-Kinetically* affected by *all* the gears. For instance, your value system (Gear 2) affects your decisions (Gear 6). They influence each other. When your clearly defined values, purpose, and goals are in place as set in the **Operating System-Blueprint Gear,** your decision-making power will be sharper and smarter. Business leaders in every field understand the value and importance of quick, wise decisions. Politicians and celebrities know all too well the devastating effects of one bad decision that makes the news.

Procrastination Puts Rust on Your Decision Gear 6

"Procrastination is the thief of time; collar him."

- Charles Dickens, David Copperfield

Indecision can be disempowering. Rust in your action gear can cause lost opportunity and bigger problems because a delay allows them to fester and grow. Chronic procrastination can be like an infestation of termites eating away at your foundation; you don't notice its damaging effects until it's too late. **Procrastination causes you to lose options and opportunities.** But for the purposes of this discussion, indecision, procrastinating or not making any decision really is a no-go decision. Feeling the need to wait for the perfect moment, insisting on having every fact, or holding off until you feel better are rust makers. All of these delay distractions can rust up your decision-making faculty.

Procrastination and neglect can rust up the whole works, resulting in mediocrity and frustrating outcomes/conditions!

Disempowering "Rocks" That Weigh You Down

Nobody is rock free. There will always be challenges, burdens and problems. Some rocks you can throw out; others can be reduced to manageable pebbles. But taking action depends on you. One of my early turning-point realizations came from a poster I saw on a store wall that simply said, "If it's going to be, then it's up to me." It was a wakeup call to me about *taking responsibility,* because no one was coming to reprieve me. The freedom of choice is a gift we've been given as humans. This free will is both **powerful** and **dangerous.** Just as an automobile is powerful enough to take us anywhere we want to go, it can also take out light poles, fire hydrants, and even innocent pedestrians. And so with this powerful liberty of choice comes great responsibility.

Your Level of Commitment to a Decision

Your *level of commitment* sets the amount of force that binds your decision to go for it and get it done. It is first cousin to persistence. Persistence increases the odds of reaching your successful outcomes. Your level of obligation **to yourself and to your goals and purpose** is the glue that holds you together through good times and bad. It's like holding onto a rope that leads into a fog and keeps you going in the right direction, even if you can't see exactly which direction will take you through.

Once again when you look at champions in any field you will always find this common denominator of persistence in their success formula. The following is a tiny sample of how persistence won the day and got them into the success vault.

Number of times failed:

- **Richard Branson:** 400 failed company launches
- **Sylvester Stallone:** over 1000 rejections for his "Rocky" script
- **Theodore Geisel (Dr. Seuss):** rejected 27 times, being told his work was "too different from other juveniles on the market to warrant its selling."

- **Colonel Sanders:** 900+ failures to find someone to use his fried chicken recipe
- **Steven Spielberg:** rejected two times from Southern California University Film School
- **Jack Canfield** and **Mark Victor Hansen:** 144 rejections by publishers for *Chicken Soup for The Soul*
- **Walt Disney:** 302 rejections before getting financing for Disneyland
- **Meg Cabot:** three years of rejections for *The Princess Diaries*
- **Agatha Christie:** five years of continual rejection. Her book sales have now topped $2 billion.
- **The Beatles**: dropped by their early record label, Decca: "We don't like their sound, and guitar music is on the way out."

A few years back, billionaire author of the Harry Potter series, J.K. Rowling, told the graduating class at Harvard, "You might never fail on the scale I did, but it is impossible to live without failing at something, unless you live so cautiously that you might as well not have lived at all-in which case, you fail by default."[68]

Up next are some additional viewpoints on risk vs. opportunity. There are four basic risk management techniques used in business that can also apply to personal development. They are as follows:

- Avoid risk
- Transfer risk
- Control risk
- Retain risk

Each option has its benefit and value depending on the situation in the moment. For the sake of this discussion we will think from the perspective of *controlling* it through preparation and *retaining* it as a calculated chance that is worth the price.

Risk and Opportunity:
The Other Two-Sided Coin

*"The biggest risk is not taking any risk...
In a world that's changing really quickly, the only strategy where
you're guaranteed to fail is not taking risks."*

- Mark Zuckerberg, Facebook co-founder[69]

The two sides come as a pair

So-called "failure" and risk are part of the success formula. Failures (really just outcomes or results) give you three things if you're persistent: **1.** you *gain wisdom* if you learn something, *anything,* from the loss or failure, even if it only shows you what to change; **2.** if you persist, you know you're *one step closer* to success; **3.** your tenacity *builds strength of character* for your next challenge.

Which Way Will You Go?

If you really think about it, you are given a brand <u>new opportunity every waking</u> minute. Opportunities are generated every moment, every minute, hour and day! Never in the history of time have the opportunities been so good! You could say this about any point in the human history time line, and it would still be true. And wherever you find commitment as a clue to someone's success, persistence and responsibility are always present. One of the basic principles found in Neuro-Linguistic Programming is that "choice is better than no choice," and that rule certainly applies with this gear.

When a young truck driver named Elvis Presley determined to make a record for his mom, he *decided* to go into Sun Studios in Memphis, which sparked results in a direction that had unfathomable effects in his life and the music industry. What if he had decided not to go through with that first record? About a year later, after a performance at The Grand Ole Opry, he was told to go back to driving a truck. Decisions are life changing, and the amazing thing about some decisions is that you may never know which ones are the big ones.

There's something innate in all humans that makes us want to jump higher, run faster, and break the standing record. Deep down, we all *seek fulfillment*, to be the best version of ourselves, to raise our standard of living from wherever we are. When you can, look up the following amazing adventurers. Austrian Sir Felix

Baumgartner jumped out of a helium-filled balloon from 128,000 feet above New Mexico, falling faster than the speed of sound. And then there's Ann Bancroft, the first woman to trek across both polar icecaps, and Ranulph Fiennes, now in his 70s, is considered today to be the world's greatest living explorer. He holds many endurance records before and after his heart bypass surgery, including climbing to the top of Mt. Everest at age 65. Many more human spirit stories are happening around us every day; they just don't always make the news. There is an amazing human determination story happening right now in your city or town, probably even your neighborhood.

The human spirit can come alive to such levels as to perform seeming miracles. But it all starts when you make the decision to cut from the past, live in the present moment, and decide to make the most of your talents, skills, and abilities. Think about this. Spending too much attention energy on the past and the future is like revving your engine in park: a lot of noise, exhaust fumes, and spent fuel for nothing.

Decide right now: Are you going to be an Out-stander or a Bystander?

The Speed of Your Decisions

It's been proven that one of the key characteristics of successful leaders is their ability to make decisions quickly and stick with those decisions. That's wise advice. However, you can save a lot of future grief and trouble by not being *too quick* in saying yes, and not be *too slow* in saying no. In other words there is a "sweet spot" when it comes to timing some of your choices and responses. When at the crossroads of making important decisions, make sure you have a sufficient level of knowledge about what you're deciding on, yet remain agile enough to not get bogged down in "paralysis analysis." Follow this quick rule of thumb and save much anxiety on the other side of your decisions: 1. Consider the many alternatives; 2. Get the facts and think the proposal or decision through to its end; 3. *Then move on it and don't look back.*

Smart Performance-Decision Meter

The Timing of Your Choices and Decisions

In the previous section we talked about the valued habit of making decisions quickly to avoid procrastination. There are times when hasty decisions without a moment of consideration can cause regret. This is why the more decisions you make, the better you get at it. It is an important skill that needs to be developed and worked on every day. In the book *TNT: The Power Within You*, Claude M. Bristol and Harold Sherman identify one more benefit that practicing the art of good decision-making has for you. Decision-making has a "magnetic affect" on your mind. They say, "Decision starts an immediate magnetic action in your mind, which rearranges the iron filings of your life, reassembles the broken pieces, fits them together into a new fabric, strengthens the weak spots, and gives you new vitality and resolution to do what the 'inner voice' dictates."[70]

The Wisdom of Your Decisions

By now you probably grasp that high achievers are risk takers. In between all of these examples and concepts is an important distinction between taking wise risks and taking foolish, or even dangerous, chances. Author Paul McKenna defines it well when he says, "Too many people stop themselves from doing something because it seems 'too risky.'" But professional risk-takers aren't necessarily braver, just more prepared. McKenna identifies two types of risk as "those that are imposed on us from the outside and those we choose to take on for ourselves in hopes of greater or accelerated reward."[71] Wise decisions, depending on the magnitude of the consequence, need some amount of skilled evaluation, but you may not have every detail ahead of time.

When you're faced with important decisions, make sure your emotions are in control and not off the scale in either direction. In this case, the short pause to regain composure works well. Remember what we said about emotion being behind the steering wheel, while logic and clear thinking take the passenger seat. That extra time can make the difference in the quality of your big-ticket decisions!

Having said that, there are times when an intense negative emotional experience can actually serve as a turning point in your favor. That is, IF you use the firepower of vowing to "never let this happen again" and IF your Values, Purpose, and Goals are clear and positive. In conclusion, the speed, timing and wisdom of your decisions get better with conscious, intentional practice, which is why those who make many high-level decisions in the workforce are in leadership positions.

And finally, when you make a **Decision-Choice (Gear 6),** you drive the **7th Gear,** outer **Action!** *It's time to shift into the 7th Gear!*

<u>Worth Remembering</u>

- **Until you decide to stop trying and applying, you are never defeated.**

- **Really think on this one! You** *always* **have choices even if you don't like the choices in front of you in the moment. Therefore, you are not a victim as long as you exercise your first point of power, Decision-Choice, Gear 6.**

- **Some decisions can be put off to some point in the future, but all decisions** *happen* **in the now moment; that's why it's called the first point of power.**

- **Whatever you** *decide* **to take responsibility for gives you control, and after all, isn't that what you want?**

- **You won't** *get* **change until you** *make* **the change first in Gears 1-6.**

- **Remember a time when you wrestled over a decision and then felt a wave of relief once you made it?**

- Sometimes it only takes one decision to change your life. Think back on your life history, and you will find one. See how powerful decisions can be?

- A lack of decision *is* a decision.

- A decision made is the conception of action.

- A firm decision dissolves procrastination, which is the enemy of choice.

- Summary: When your <u>Decisions and Choices</u> change, your results and conditions change.

<u>Worth Doing</u>

- Begin building your decision fitness by *practicing* the art of well-timed, wiser decisions. The more you do it, the better you get at it.

- Ask yourself what one decision you could make today that would move you toward just one of your goals. Build this into a daily habit.

- Accept responsibility for everything that happens to you. It keeps your hands on the steering wheel of control.

- Keep possession of your decisions; that is, don't give them over to someone else.

- Delay important decisions if you're angry or upset.

- Practice the "Ben Franklin T" on borderline decisions: draw a "T" on paper and list pros on one side and cons on the other, then tally.

- Exercising the popular technique of "sleeping on it" has merit for difficult and important decisions. Turn it over to the subconscious mind. Giving your subconscious a firm "order" before bed has been tested to work better than a soft, timid question.

- Commit to being a student, not a follower.

- Practice the art of taking informed risks. Quickly gathering information about a pending decision helps you make wiser choices, otherwise known as "informed risks."

- Decide right now—are you going to be a Bystander or an Outstander?

DECISION-CHOICE POINT Gear 6 influences and directs your...

Outer Gear

Gear •7

ACTION: Second Point of Power

"If you don't make things happen, then things will happen to you."

- Anonymous

EFFECT

Action is traction, IF you're in gear! Recall in the preface when I asked if you are ready to get your life into a higher gear? Well this is it; this is your call to action—High Gear 7! All of the previous gears create a sort of traction mat for the 7th Gear that allows you to move out and move ahead. With all the previous gears in place and tuned up, your odds of reaching your goals and getting the kinds of results you're seeking go up, up, up!

In the business world there's a saying that "nothing happens until first a sale is made." And that's exactly what the 6th and 7th Gears are about: "making the sale."

321

First you make the *decision* to go for it (Gear 6), and then you make the ***organized action*** plan to move on that decision (Gear 7)! Action is THE gear that determines whether or not you succeed or "fail" at anything and everything. All the energy of the previous gears *must* pass through the Action Gear.

There are two major dynamic forces at work with this gear

1) **This is the place where thoughts, ideas, and decisions transition *out from* the mental-spiritual realm into physical, outward world as something visible and tangible.**

2) **This is the gear that *makes contact* with the Effect, outcomes, results, experiences and conditions. Call it the manifestation gear.**

All of the previous gears are meant to *get you to this point* to take action. But not just action, but more effective action, **action with traction!**

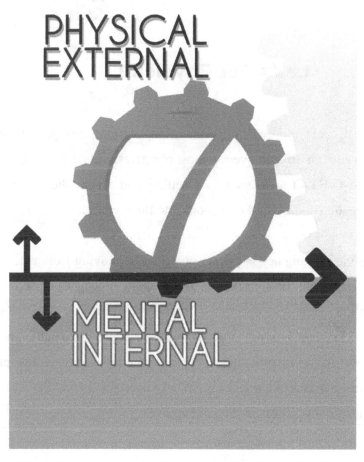

The Conversion Point into the Visible!

Let's Get Physical!

With all of the previous gears humming along, turning this gear should now be easier, with enough drive to overrun most obstacles. This is the place where your **PERFORM-O-STAT** *delivers* on its setting and where the invisible mental-emotional realm *connects* and transitions into the physical, external realm.

Most of us view taking action toward our goals as moving from where we are to where the goal is. But taking action is like having a rope around the goal, and you are pulling the roped goal towards you at the same time you are moving towards it. You can't see it yet because of the distance, yet if you keep pulling on the *belief rope,* the goal will eventually appear. This is where the gravitational phenomena of *accelerating acceleration* kicks in. What you want wants you. There are also two other extremely important facets of action.

The "I'll Wait Until" Trap

"Every successful person I have heard of has done the best he could with conditions as he found them, and not waited until the next year for better."

- Edgar W. Howe, 19th-century American newspaper editor

Many people get caught up in the wrong idea that you must wait until conditions are just right and then take action. Nearly all successful people, no matter what their calling, have the common habit of making decisions quickly and often. Henry Ford was a quick decision maker, and it was a factor in building his empire.

Seemingly insignificant daily actions and choices are like flash flood water that started out as little rain droplets cascading to a force to be reckoned with! Keep in mind the long-term significance of *every* action and decision, and you will minimize wasted time. When you took your first act of writing down your goals as described in **Gear 2, Operating System-Blueprint,** and put pencil to paper, you started the forces into motion, into reality. One of the best resources on the subject is Henriette Anne Klauser's book *Write It Down, Make It Happen*, which I highly recommend you add to your personal development library. Like a Hollywood movie, our lives are stories or screenplays. As Shakespeare said, "All the world's a stage." We as players all have parts, and you are the director, producer *and* player!

Starting is Half Done!

It's been reported that one of the top reasons people don't reach their goals is simply because they don't *move* on what they know they should do, by taking action. You don't want to be in that statistic! Recall the success formula from Thomas Huxley. One of the best ways to break out of that inertia is to ***demand*** of yourself that you will **commit** to applying all of these gears with **Sustained Unwavering Progress** through wiser **Daily Action Habits.** Once again, the primary purpose of the first six gears is to generate enough *cause power* to turn this **7th Gear** into action!

Transition point

The Tangent Point
– 2nd Point of Power –
Action

The Tangent Point, the 2nd Point of Power

The dictionary defines tangent as "making contact at a single point with a line, curve, surface; meeting another line, curve or surface." Tangent point is where a piano hammer hits the string, or a tennis ball smacks the racket.

Note: All of the Gears have tangent points of contact as each **cog** makes contact to the other. When you step into the ocean, you are connected to the entire ocean and to all connected bodies of water.

This is called the point of power because *changing your future begins in the present moment, right here, right now.* The first six gears' mission is to get you to this point with enough spark and firepower. This is where you carry out the *organized plan of action* you assembled in **Gear 2.** Action gets you into new areas of opportunity you would never know by just staying in your comfort zone on the couch. "Success breeds success." Action-breeds-action, if only on a small scale, and every action adds up. What counts is what resources you have at the ready right now! That is why **Gears 6 and 7** are called **points of power**. Power to change, improve, advance into your vision, purpose, and goals faster! You are the pitcher *and* batter, the ship's captain *and* navigator.

Where the Rubber Meets the Road!

Action is the *tangent point of power* because it isn't the past or future; it's only in the now. It's called the point of power because it's the one place you have absolute command and control! Never earlier or later, but right now, you have your hand

328

on the steering wheel and foot on the gas! In the *present moment* you have direct access to all possibilities and infinite potential!

Most of us are aware of the importance of taking action in varying degrees, at different times and in different situations. Even so, our awareness of its value and importance can drop out of sight when we get caught up in distractions. There will always be distractions, but without the *sense of urgency* to get back on track, we can end up majoring in minor things. Let's not confuse effective action with activity. Effective action happens when it fits in with the other gears in delivering outcomes and results, especially the kind of results I know you're after.

The Residual Power of Persistence

Once you've gained **momentum** on a task or habit pattern, have you ever noticed how it seems easier to continue on, taking less energy to get going again? If you start an exercise regimen and you successfully get to the gym four days a week, for example, you have built up the "flywheel effect." The flywheel effect is similar to a grinding stone or bicycle. Once its speed and momentum are built up, you can exert less effort. The wheel continues moving on its own without any outside force—for a time.

If ever there was a real secret of secrets, this is it: YOUR thoughts, feelings, and actions focused in the ***now*** moment is the zone where you have control of your results, outcomes, and destiny! Happiness, health, and wealth begins right here. This is the MASTER Combination that unlocks that safe you saw earlier. So it's not just "according to your faith be it unto you", but also, "according to your action be it unto you."

MOMENTUM

Persistence Power

> *"Don't wait until you're good before you start.*
> *Start where you are, and then get good."*

- Louis E. Tice[72]

A "Law of Attraction" By Action

Once you get going, you gain **momentum;** the giant heavy wheel runs over obstacles that, at a slower velocity, would have slowed you down or derailed your forward movement. A locomotive can't slow down in time for a car stuck on the tracks; it just plows through whatever gets in its way. Another benefit of momentum is that new and different opportunities are attracted to you. The spinning wheel concept creates a *gravitational pull* that has drawing power. Someone says, "She's going places!" Athletes and entertainers get on a roll, and one opportunity leads to another. A successful actor or entertainer gets more gigs because they're out there moving and shaking. CEOs get CEO positions.

In the world of electronics, when a voltage and current run through a copper coil, a magnetic field is generated. This is how giant electro magnets can lift junk cars in a scrap yard. The same applies to you when you are in *mental* or *physical* action—you generate a "current" through your "coil" (Action Gear), and that creates a magnetic field that draws opportunities.

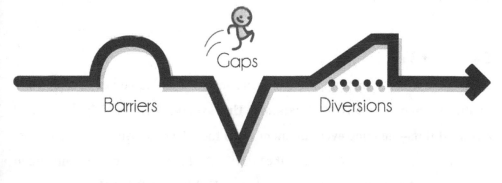

Movement is critical to our health and affects our mood and mindset. When you're bogged down on or feeling stuck, just getting up and taking a walk can change your outlook and perception. As mentioned many times before, the 7 Gears have a forward movement to them, but also have a reverse influencing effect. Just taking action, any action, creates a lubricating effect on any one or all of the six previous gears. *Persistence Power* is the engine power that keeps the propeller moving and the airplane aloft.

> *"Great works are performed, not by strength, but by perseverance."*
>
> - Samuel Johnson, *Rasselas*

Daily Action Habit (DAH)

Don't expect anyone to do for you what you need to be doing yourself. Daily action habits are patterns of behavior, and we ALL have them. Our Daily Action Habits either empower or disempower. We are either moving toward our goals or not; there's no in-between.

SUP-DAH memct!

SAY WHAT?

What in the world is that supposed to mean, and why should you even care?

SUPDAH memct stands for **Sustained Unwavering Progress** through **Daily Action Habits—**making every moment count today! The Japanese have a saying, "Kaizen," which means "seize the day." And my version is **Sustained Unwavering Progress through Daily Action Habits: SUP-DAH!**

Whenever you take a closer look at champions in any area of life, you will find this common personal characteristic. They all have developed a level of commitment to **advance** and **progress** by grabbing anything that is an improvement to what they do. It means dedication to being the best at what you do, whether it's sports, medicine, or public service. Successful entertainers and winning athletes know the value of this type of commitment. And if you're serious about making exciting change and progress, you need to *want* to be the best at what you do. If you can't feel it in your bones, then something's wrong and you need to go back to the **Operating System-Blueprint Gear 2** and re-evaluate your goals, purpose, and identity. You must be committed to **Sustained Unwavering Progress**, another **sine qua non.** In today's increasing level of competition, having a full-out, no-holds-barred commitment to **Sustained Unwavering Progress** is a *must*! If you take nothing else away from this book, then grab this one and run with it! I believe this alone is your ticket to gaining the competitive edge you need, notwithstanding all 7 gears' collective power.

The Power of Accumulation Principle

Every micro-mini bit of progress counts and adds up; any improvement, no matter how small, is being on track, and it's to be counted as forward momentum. Ben Franklin once described the two qualities of perseverance and energy as a "personal power" that will assure success. Sometimes our efforts seem to go nowhere or feel like a waste, but that viewpoint can be deceptive because every action adds up. A tree does not get chopped down by one swing of the axe; it requires multiple swings. As simple as all this sounds, it's where real change and real progress takes place, and it's easy to forget that you must pass through a certain number of "axe cutting chops" to get to the *last chop* that proves you've made it. Einstein once said that the greatest mathematical discovery of all time is compound interest, and so the proven principle of sustained incremental efforts over time can have a huge compounding impact at some point in your future. Burn this mantra into your consciousness: **"Day by day in every way, I am committed to Sustained Unwavering Progress through my Daily Action Habits –** making every moment count today!" **SUPDAH** *memct!*

Sticking with it has another benefit; it actually starts to <u>feel good</u>. Making progress, even one small forward movement, delivers a seed of confidence that affects your self-esteem. If ever there was something to have an addiction to, this is it! Psychologists and researchers working in the area of depression and suicide prevention have determined that in addition to taking action, laughter, and running, the act of completing a task causes the brain to releases endorphins, also known as "runner's high." <u>Completing steps and tasks feels good</u>! And isn't that what we all want—to feel good?

It's been said that the definition of success is "the progressive realization toward worthwhile goals." I would add, however, that "finishing what you begin" more completely defines it.

It Isn't All Physical

Daily habits of *mental* focus

Habit patterns are internal and are not so easy to change once they gain momentum. Ask a smoker to quit or a nail biter to stop the habit immediately, and they will likely tell you in no uncertain terms that it's not as easy as just deciding to stop. Focusing on what you *do* want every day and not giving in to thinking about what you *don't* want can become a habit worth engraining into your consciousness through segmented repetition. You will advance in your **eight goal areas** by using these 7 gears. **Make it a habit to apply at least one of these gears every day.**

Research on the subject of habits shows that a new action habit sustained for 21–31 days will give you the momentum that carries you along thereafter. It doesn't have to be a physical habit such as getting up one hour earlier every day. You can build **mental habits** that are empowering, like practicing Sudoku or a memory puzzle every day. Think of a new empowering mental habit or something that improves your mind, such as learning three new words in French every week. Better yet, add three new useful facts or bits of information about your profession. Remember, everything adds up in your favor when you're committed to **Sustained Unwavering Progress, SUP-DAH**.

The Flywheel Effect

"To every action there is always opposed an equal reaction."

- Isaac Newton

Sustained Unwavering Progress through

Daily Action Habits

As you can see in the graphic, the ACTION GEAR is depicted as a flywheel, big and heavy. **Not so easy to *get* going, but easier to *keep* going.**

Physical: Daily Action Habits

Have you ever heard of a Kugel ball? It's a fun novelty made of a large granite ball that's supported underneath by a thin layer of high pressure water. The large stone ball can weigh thousands of pounds, and yet human hands can push it and spin it. If you *keep* pushing, it gains momentum, and pretty soon the ball is moving at a high velocity! This is how the **Flywheel Effect** works; harder to start; easier to keep going. It's what happens when exercising **Daily Action Habits**. But in order to get to this level of persistence and momentum, you must be more than just interested; you must have a *passion* and *commitment* to follow through on your goals and objectives. You must be committed to **Sustained Unwavering Progress (SUP)** through **Daily Action Habits (DAH)!**

We've done the *lights* and the *camera*; now it's *action* time. But focused action MUST be a consistent, daily, habit to make the kind of progress I know you're after. That's the *DAH in* **Sustained Unwavering Progress**—MAKE EVERY MOMENT COUNT TODAY!

Mental/Emotional: Daily Action Habits

The world is always evolving and changing. We explained how **operating systems get "bugs"** and at times need fixes and updates. The same kind of attention applies to our **Daily Action Habits** because what has worked in the past may not work today. You must be vigilant and look at your "dashboard" for feedback on whether or not you are getting the results you want. Keep what works, reject what doesn't, and add something new if it's better. Upgrading new, improved habits is not easy or comfortable, but it is worth it. It's also another one of those sine qua non decision points if you're serious about making lasting quantum leaps in getting to where you want to be. You must change out disempowering habits for ones required for your success; there's no way around it. The subconscious has set old habits in place by repetition and programming. The aircraft industry constantly inspects and changes out parts and is always running inspections for defects. Your body is changing out most of its cells at the rate of millions per second. Over 50 million of your cells just changed out while you were reading these last two sentences! You can't change a car tire by simply tugging on the wheel until it comes off. You have to run through a change routine. You jack the car up, remove the lug nuts, then pull off the tire, etc. Improving your daily action habits requires an upgrade routine as well. Go back to Gear 2 and make sure you internalize and apply every reprogramming step called out. Finally, I must again emphasize the importance of *internalizing*, and *personalizing* not only Gear 2, but *all* the gears as *your* total new upgraded 7-gear success system.

We also talked about the importance of exercising sincere, **heartfelt gratitude**. Well, this is where it applies best. As you assemble your most beneficial set of daily action habits, make sure you include this one. In other words, find something, if only *one* **thing,** every day that you are grateful or thankful for. One way to engrain and train your *habit-making machine* to run with momentum is to pick a time during the day when you focus on just being grateful. In addition to the times when the feeling comes over you because of an event or experience, use neuro-linking. For example, every time you reach for a doorknob or climb stairs, think of an empowering thought habit. Some of the best times are when you first wake up on your way to brush your teeth or take a shower, and again at night before going to bed.

Delays/Diversions: Sneaky Time Stealers and Time Warpers

Recall that we saw how our emotions and strong feelings can cause **distraction** if not bridled, and they can pull us off our schedule, many times without us realizing it until days or weeks later. Diversions can be **physical, emotional, and mental**.

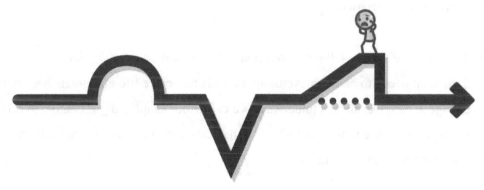

Getting **pulled off schedule** of the actions you know you should take can be deceptive because this can sneak up on you and usually comes at you either subtly or in the form of some "emergency." It's important to know that action steps don't have to be big. The old adage applies here: "Inch by inch, anything's a cinch; by the yard, it's hard."

SELF-DISCIPLINE II: Is There Any Guarantee?

Self-discipline and momentum are the best weapons against barriers, gaps, and diversions to your goals and objectives. You thought we were done going over the subject of discipline? Not just yet. It's so important that it applies to this gear too.

Besides, death, taxes, and liquor stores, there are no guarantees in life. Yet the closest thing to a guarantee of achievement or success is that boring word again— *discipline*. It's self-discipline to persist and never give up. Persistence is staying IN gear. Ideally, it's utilizing all 7 gears. When you apply self-discipline to persist through any barriers, gaps, or diversions, you also are taking the steering wheel of responsibility, and that keeps you in control! It's worth the temporary discomfort of getting up off the couch, heading to the gym, making the call, or whatever you know you need to do. More valuable even than talent or skill is the habit pattern of persistence in assuring that you reach your goals. **Self-discipline is the best warrantee you can own.**

In this instance we are talking about discipline to *stay with* *your plan of action*, and *do* what needs to be done. Actually, there is one more life guarantee, and that is change. Change is always underway; we can either adapt and use change to our advantage, or ignore it and get kicked to the curb. Applying these gears will help to eliminate that kind of setback.

Self-discipline has not only been called "the master key to success;" it's credited as being **the compelling force** that separates high achievers from the masses. We talked about the importance of self-discipline's effect on our **Motivation to Action (MTA),** and it is just as important when considering the working elements of this gear, **Gear 7, Action**. So when we talk about self-discipline, we're really talking about persistence and perseverance. That means keeping your visualized goals in front of you and being committed to *Sustained Unwavering Progress* through your **Daily Action Habits—SUPDAH.** In addition to having your **Operating System** and **Blueprint** plans in place, seek out good role models who are leading the field you are in or want to be in. Doing this gives you proof positive that if they can do it, then so can you. If you were to get in front of your role models right now and ask, "How did you get to the top?" you'd find that every answer would include this viewpoint and perspective: "I reached a point where I said to myself, if they can do it, so can I!"

Overpowering Inertia: Divide and Conquer

There are a number of clever techniques for overcoming inertia and getting yourself motivated enough to get off the couch and get going. And you may want to look those up; however, if you've really invested yourself into these 7 gears, you shouldn't need any motivating tricks. Your motivation level, **MTA,** will already be fired up for all the deeper, more compelling reasons called out in this book. It's fine to have a working knowledge of swimming and horseback riding, but at some point you have to *get in* the water or *get on* the horse.

A Jet Plane Has No Rearview Mirror

Because jets and airplanes only go forward, they don't need a rearview mirror. Except for glancing back to think on lessons learned, *you* don't need a rearview mirror either. Develop the mindset of jet-plane thinking! Focus on the present, moving forward and upward because the past is done, and your today is your future. "*Forgetting what is behind and straining toward what is ahead, I press on toward the goal to win the prize*" (Phil. 3:13).[73] As mentioned earlier, none of us is a solo act. I hope that some of the contents and perspectives in this book will be of use to you. *The 7 Gears* is the distillation of the best of what I've learned over several years of trial and error. It's Go time; it's your move!

Worth Remembering

- It's not about how much you do; it's what you deliver and how effective your actions have been today. Activity and productivity aren't the same thing.

- If you're playing the waiting game to get started when conditions are just right, the odds will be stacked against you.

- All the previous gears are meant to get you to this point, to make smart action pay off.

- Remember what was said about the power of asking? Asking is a form of action that is often overlooked. Ask more, and be surprised how it was worth it. You can verify this by thinking back to a life-changing question you once asked.

- Any form of action puts fear in retreat.

- Your Daily Action Habits (DAH) are shaping and predicting the quality of your future.

- When you procrastinate, you throw away precious time, and opportunities sneak right past you.

- The world will pay you for what you know IF it's combined with what you deliver in value. You've got to have both!

- Summary: When your <u>Action</u> changes, your experiences and conditions change.

<u>Worth Doing</u>

- Commit to a mind and body exercise habit because you need it to build emotional/mental health and physical vitality.

- Ask yourself: "What is my level of commitment to be the best at what I do?" That is, if you're really serious about accomplishing your goals.

- Don't try to stop a bad habit, but rather *trade* up for a more empowering one, *exchanging* one for one. That's how you make Sustained Unwavering Progress.

- Ask yourself, "Is what I'm acting on moving me forward?" Keep what works. Throw out what doesn't. Seek improvement. Repeat every day until it's conditioned into you as a power habit.

- Having a trusted accountability partner is statistically proven to dramatically ensure you follow through!

- Don't wait for conditions to be just right. Start where you are, invest what you have, do what you can, and don't wait for "just one more thing" to get going.

- You must shift out of neutral and into gear (apply) to make any advice and guidance work for you.

- Commit to SUPDAH -<u>Sustained Unwavering Progress</u> through your <u>Daily Action Habits,</u> making every moment count! *It's your closest thing to a guarantee to success* when it's running on the S.M.A.R.T.E.R goal track.

- According to your *ACTION* be it unto you—not just faith. You need both.

Your Action Gear 7 creates your...

PART THREE

EFFECT

SPECIAL EFFECTS

Outcomes, Results & Conditions
(oh my!)—The Effect Side

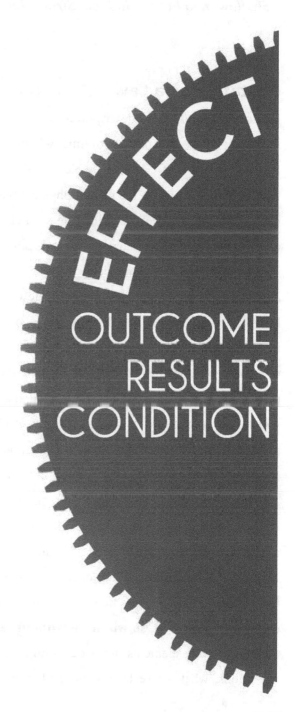

EFFECT

OUTCOME
RESULTS
CONDITION

"Shallow men believe in luck. Strong men believe in cause and effect."

- Ralph Waldo Emerson

Gestation as a Law

Up to this point, most descriptions of the process of Cause and Effect have indirectly inferred the passage of time, whether it's five seconds or five years. That fits with the Law of Gestation, which says all things take time to manifest from their beginning. And on the mental/physical plane, there is a measurable time lag between causes and their resulting effects. Yet the Cause and Effect Law functions on all three planes of existence: mental, physical, and spiritual. There are some who believe there is no time delay at the spiritual level between cause and effect, as suggested in the complete 7 Gear overview graphic. A connection at the spiritual level exists as inseparable to any stage or place, without the need for any interceding elements. Any further discussion is beyond the scope and intention of this book. We don't have to fully understand the details of how satellite radio or a cell phone works to use them to our benefit and enjoyment. We only need to know which button to push or what knob to turn. And all of us have experienced God's power and mysterious ways, whether we acknowledge it or not.

Whatever you want **externally** in effects, outcomes and results, you must first become on the **inside** where the real change must begin. Haven't you ever reached a goal and said to yourself, "Hey, if I can do this, what else can I do?" Recall that **Universal Laws intersect** and operate within common parameters. The Law of Correspondence is one example, asserting, "As above, so below; **as it is within (internal Gears 1-6), so will it be without (external).**" All of the **7 gears** and their supporting elements are a cascading succession of stages, processes, and operations, what we've been calling "factors." This is so important it's worth repeating: you don't have to create these factor-gears; it's more a matter of lubricating and repairing what has always been there. Consider **the 7 Gears** not as an invention, but rather a discovery of what has always been there waiting to be systematically aligned and activated. They're already in place, ready to go to work for you if you apply them with your unique fingerprint of individuality. You have always been using them individually, if only by default, but maybe not realizing their importance in getting control over your **outcomes** and **conditions**. You've always had your "ruby slippers" waiting and ready to lead you to a more rewarding, fulfilling life, the life I believe our Creator intended for us.

"Obviously, then, to improve your luck and become more successful, you must change your ingrained customary behavior."

- Bernard Gittelson[74]

What Condition Is Your Condition In?

Many people try to change only what they outwardly see, not understanding where change really begins. They rely just on **Gear 6 (decide)** and **Gear 7 (act)** to get the job done, because even action without direction will take you somewhere. If you're serious about finding every opportunity that may benefit you and your loved ones, then all 7 gears need to be internalized and applied.

James Allen explains in, *As a Man Thinketh,* that "a man is continually revolting against an effect without, while all the time he is nourishing and preserving its cause in his heart."[75] Most people do not understand that most of our outcomes and conditions are under our control. It's been phrased many ways, but the bottom line is this: the way to mastery of your experiences is through the decision-making gift of directing your conscious and subconscious mind. And you must also get your conscious and subconscious working in harmony instead of resisting each other, as odd as that sounds. We now know that the conscious and subconscious minds speak different dialects. The conscious mind **speaks "logic,"** making inferences and judgments; this is found in Gears 1, 2, 4, and 6. The subconscious mind, however, understands **emotions, repetitive input, and images** (Gears 1, 3, and 5). Intense desire, sensory-rich imaging, and repetition are the universal translators. **The 7 Gears** are simply the ways and means to create the level of influence you must have to make it happen.

You Need More Than One Gear to Handle the Terrain

The difference now is that you are equipped with better tools and the knowledge to do something about it. With this new knowledge and expanded perspective on how to increase control over your circumstances, there are no excuses left. You have a right and a responsibility to go forward, to get back out there and make a difference, a new and bigger difference!

You Are the Change Agent to Your Future!

You become the **change agent** to getting what you want by:

1. Choosing to take responsibility (Gear 6) and, therefore, control.
2. Having clear, well-fit goals, values, purpose and identity, as set in Gear 2.
3. Having the motivation to make it happen (Gears 2, 3, 4 & 5).
4. Having your planning and approach laid out (Gear 2).
5. Building up your knowledge and skill through constant learning of what works and what doesn't (Gears 1, 4, and Outcome Effect Gear).
6. Being committed to persist and make it happen (Gears 3, 4, 5, 6 & 7).

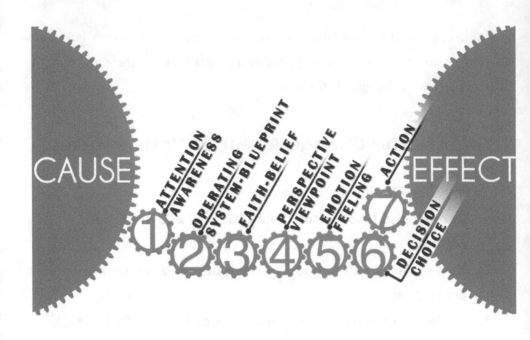

CAUSE — ATTENTION / AWARENESS (1) — OPERATING SYSTEM-BLUEPRINT (2) — FAITH-BELIEF (3) — PERSPECTIVE / VIEWPOINT (4) — EMOTION / FEELING (5) — (6) — DECISION / CHOICE — ACTION (7) — EFFECT

"*Your time is limited, so don't waste it living someone else's life. Don't be trapped by dogma, which is living with the results of other people's thinking. Don't let the noise of others' opinions drown out your own inner voice. And most important, have the courage to follow your heart and intuition. They somehow already know what you truly want to become. Everything else is secondary.*"

- Steve Jobs[76]

If much of this seems easy, why then don't we just do it? One reason is not being committed with enough emotional energy in the moment to step over the comfort zone wall built of all those fear-laden bricks we talked about. And, because it's easier to let up and fall prey to the barriers, gaps and diversions that confront us every day. Or we just don't really want it bad enough; it's just so easy to take it easy!

Barriers, Gaps & Diversions Will Always Be There

You can start out going to the gym and hold to that discipline for a couple of weeks, and then SOMETHING comes up. Your sister from out of town comes to visit, for example, and you get out of your routine, and then another diversion, and another, and so on. And before you realize it, six weeks have gone by since your last visit to the gym!

It's easy to stop pedaling or stop rowing, if only for just one break. Like weightlifting, challenging experiences build strength when you take a systematic approach. Just as a bodybuilder gains strength and form by working out through a series of weight-based machines, the challenging events and circumstances you encounter can build strength—**strength of character**. Extreme negative events don't have to pull you down to the point of being incapacitated anymore. Your intentional use of the 7 Gears in good working order can reduce, if not eliminate, most of the debilitating outcomes and conditions you may bump into. <u>The "workout" of challenging events will strengthen you and qualify you for a higher standard of living.</u> This is how you qualify for the "things on the higher shelf" - the rewarding life of having more of your goals and dreams realized.

We can't directly command our heart rate to speed up, but we can cause it to speed up *indirectly* by running or some form of physical exertion. We don't always have *direct* control over our circumstances, but we do have the empowering gift of choice (Gear 6) that allows us to decide how we think, respond and use our 7 Gears. Recall James Allen's words in *As a Man Thinketh:* "A man cannot directly choose his circumstances, but he can choose his thoughts, and so indirectly, yet surely, shape his circumstances."[77]

At the end of the last chapter in **Worth Doing,** Cog said to *ask if what you're acting on is working. Keep what works, seek improvement, and throw out what doesn't.* Repeat this every day until it's conditioned into you.

The 80/20 Rule

The 80/20 Rule is one of the areas where you can really empower your time and efforts towards reaching your dreams and goals.

Pareto's Principle

Italian economist Vilfredo Pareto observed that 80 percent of his country's wealth and power was controlled by 20 percent of his countrymen. The real discovery is that so many things today fit that ratio. For example:

- **80** percent of all university research grants are obtained by **20** percent of the professors. (I can vouch for this one!).
- **80** percent of your success will arrive in the last **20** percent of the time you invest—if you persist.
- **80** percent of software problems are caused by **20** percent of bugs (Remember what Gear 2 is about?)
- **80** percent of restaurant menu selections come from **20** percent of the items.
- **80** percent of your company's sales come from **20** percent of your sales team.

You and I also have an **80/20 rule** running in each of our **eight life goal areas.** So how can we use this to our advantage? Concentrate on the top 20 percent of what's most essential and find ways to leverage that 20 percent. Invest more of your time and energy on the 20 percent of your proven skills and strengths. By converting this to your best 20 percent of personal strengths, you can leverage what you're best at. This habit alone can do wonders in boosting your effectiveness in reaching your outcomes and goals because you've cut wasted time! I recommend you check out author Richard Koch's book *Living the 80/20 Way: Work Less, Worry Less, Succeed More, Enjoy More*. He does a great job of delving into the principle and explains how you can use it to your advantage for better life outcomes and results.[78]

Divide and Conquer

Recall that if you're struggling with making real progress in a certain goal area, you should **divide** the goal in such a way that you change a 50/50 probability to an 80/20 chance of reaching the goal, or any percentage better than 50/50. The object is to increase the odds of winning more successes, no matter how small, and harvest the feeling of confidence as **proof to your subconscious mind**. Building up enough small success paves the way for bigger successes.

By now you can see that behind every outcome, result or condition, there is a cause set in motion. More importantly, you have been given the gift of choice to **activate** and **apply** enough tools and resources to build a magnificent, rewarding life.

Flight Path to Your Future—Your Destiny

Having made it this far, you now possess an expanded vantage point that you can leverage. You now know what's really possible for you! Your persistence in staying with it will now pay off. A good friend of mine recently completed his tour of duty in the Army, and I asked him, "Well, how was it?" He replied, "It was a million-dollar experience I wouldn't pay a dime to go through again!" The old axiom still applies here: make sure you enjoy the experience along the way to your dreams and goals. If you are staying true to your clearly defined purpose and values, and are making progress, even if it's small, you should feel the satisfaction of it all because you understand that everything and everyone counts in moving you forward. If you're unhappy or miserable in your life journey, more often than not, something's wrong or out of whack. It most likely traces back to **Operating System-Blueprint (Gear 2)**.

Steps Are Passive Mini Platforms, and Gears Are Dynamic

In the introduction, we began by pointing out the differences between the popular concept of steps and the 7 Gears. Steps are passive mini-platforms, and Gears are **Cogno-Kinetic,** moving energy along. I hope you can see how the gears <u>contain energy and movement</u> and are more than just passive building blocks or steps. You internalize the dynamic, interactive factors that are filled with their own energy when you infuse them with yours.

The Importance of Alignment

Have you ever experienced what it's like to have your back out of alignment, or your car's steering pulling to the left when you take your hands off the steering wheel? A sputtering car engine or a relationship that's out of alignment are conditions we all would rather avoid. For example, if your Goals are not aligned with your core Beliefs, Values and Identity, then your confidence and mindset suffer, and mediocrity and frustration take over. Using the gear analogy, it's like the teeth or the cogs are missing, or they are worn or grinding because of being out of alignment.

Synchronicity

Being "in sync" or "in the flow" is when things are going well for you, and everything just clicks. The Cause-to-Effect process involves an **ongoing universal flow of energy**. To obtain the maximum power flow with minimal loss, there **must be alignment**. In the world of mechanics, we want maximum transfer of power from (power plant) engine to wheels. It's the same in the internal, mental/emotional realm and the efficient functioning of our operating system. Your goals, values, and beliefs must not be in conflict; they need to be in harmony.

Have you been at a railroad crossing when one of those extra-long trains with 99 cars is passing by? The engineers place extra engines in the middle and at the rear of the length of cars. In order for the power of the engines to do the work of moving the cars along, each engine must be in sync with the others, or else each power source will work against itself and cancel out the combined transfer of power. The systematic operation of the 7 Gears operates under the same type of energy transfer rules. If one or more gears are out of sync, the other gears will be affected.

> *"If the strongest horse in the team would go ahead, he cannot, if all the rest hold back."*
>
> - Abraham Lincoln[79]

Making the *Most* of *The 7 Gears* for *Your* Best Outcomes, Results, and Conditions!

The six core objectives of this book are for you to:

1. Raise your <u>awareness</u> level of what the 7 Gears are and how they can serve you better;
2. <u>Build</u> the 7 Gears to YOUR specifications;
3. <u>Align</u> the gears for maximum energy and power transfer;
4. <u>Activate</u> and <u>apply</u> every gear, every waking moment;
5. <u>Sustain</u> and <u>commit</u> to continue running and upgrading each and every gear;
6. <u>Share</u> what *resonates* and *works* for you,

...so that you really can tap into the infinite storehouse of exciting possibilities and manifest the Effects and Results of a greater quality of life for you and those around you!

Holistic practitioners say that the cure for healing most of our maladies, diseases, and problems is found within ourselves, that our Creator has placed an inborn, miraculous healing capability within us. Doctors have accumulated enough evidence to show that a patient's recovery depends in large part on his attitude, outlook, or belief. The remedy and the cause coexist. **Our outer world of circumstances and conditions has been characterized as a manifestation of our inner world**. At this point, you should realize that most visible, outward conditions and circumstances are NOT the main cause, but rather trace back to internal, imperceptible starting points. And it's the awareness, understanding, alignment, and application of these 7 gears that will put much more horsepower into the so-called Law of Attraction. It puts a supercharger on your engine.

Lee Iacocca is an American businessman known for engineering the design of the Ford Mustang and for contributing to much of Ford's success during his tenure with Ford Motor Company. Iacocca was fired by Henry Ford II, despite the fact that the company posted a $2 billion profit that year, for what he termed "personal reasons." Iacocca's wife asked him what he was going to do about it. That's when Iacocca determined to show Mr. Ford what he could do at his competitor, Chrysler. After taking the helm, he revived the Chrysler Corporation in the 1980s.

So now, having read most of this book and learned what the key factors as gears can do for you, *what are **you** going to do about it?*

Be Aware

Be aware that some people will see the results of your new, empowered operating system and will chalk it up to luck or call your advantages "unfair!" But you will know better. You will be able to smile, knowing the truth, the durable truth of *The 7 Gears between Cause and Effect!*

It's been said that "luck is where preparation meets opportunity," and that's the kind of luck I believe in, because **you** can influence outcomes and end results to your favor. **You** shift out of default (neutral) and into deliberate design (in gear). At this point, most of the reasons for success, failure, and the invisible factors that influence the lives of us all should no longer be a mystery or credited solely to the hand of fate. You now possess the knowledge to control and influence 7 key gear-factors between the iron law of Cause and Effect! You now have the tools and techniques, through each gear, to get the end result you're after. **It's time to climb and connect your best opportunity and potential to exciting goals and outcomes!**

The "SECRET SAUCE"

In Part One, we said that the *Primary* **Cause** side is made up of Infinite Energy and Infinite Intelligence and that we don't create its power; we tap into it through alignment and resonance. The point is that **we** *always* **have access** to the Cause side of the Cause and Effect principle. And through wisdom, we can direct its flow into fantastic outcomes, results, and life experiences. Every waking moment, *we choose* to run our Gears by *default* or by purposeful *design*. Using these 7 gears comes down to giving you enhanced **leverage and power** to alter the law of averages to experiencing greater rewards and opportunities, if you systematically activate and align them. You should now have the "house advantage!" Take these seed-thought ideas and concepts with you, plant them in your mental garden, and watch them grow! Without having met you personally, **I know what you want: to feel good, to be happy, healthy, and wealthy, to be more effective in your endeavors, and to make forward progress** on each of your eight goal areas. Am I close?

The **barriers, gaps, and diversions** between you and your goals can all be conquered to get you from where you are to where you really want to be. And they serve you by building strength of character and resilience, something all champions have inside. Every person travels a multitude of pathways in life. We may have many commonalities but we all traverse different paths at different times. In the book *How to Succeed*, Brian Adams declares that "books are people" and "books present the opportunity of meeting great minds in the past and present."[80] This includes the wisdom of Shakespeare, God's word, the reasoning of Plato, the philosophy of Socrates, and many more. If you would model the wise ones, then start building your own personal library. With today's technology, it's easier than ever before to build an e-book library and have it all at your fingertips. As mentioned in the preface of this book, we've all been dealt a certain hand of cards at the game table of life. Through our endowed six faculties, we've been gifted the opportunity and capability to create, produce and deliver significant value to others and ourselves. What's easy to forget is that while we were dealt that first hand, every day of our life thereafter, *we have a new hand each day to play*.

And now let's see the whole picture again:

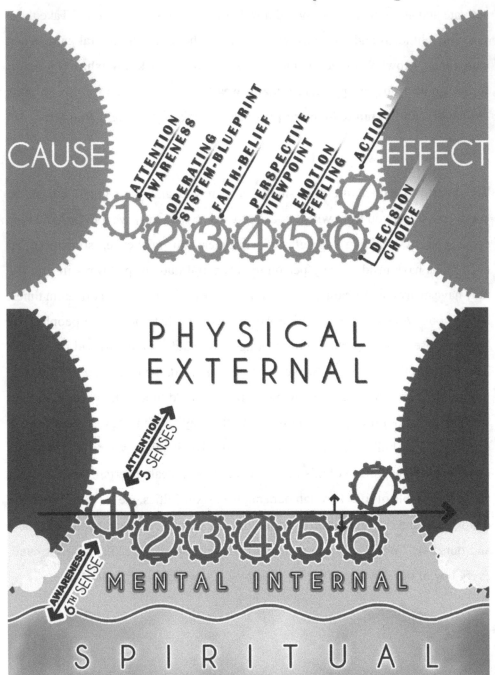

Worth Remembering

- The 7 gears augment each other to build a greater whole system than each gear by itself.

- It's when you're in the valley that you test and develop your strength of character and become stronger and wiser thereafter.

- Everyone has huge potential every day, every moment. It's not something "out there;" it's right here, right now!

- There are no real failures, only results and outcomes, and YOU label the meaning of each one.

- Solutions from the past may not work on today's problem.

- All of our successes or "failures" have reasons, and those causes pass through the 7 Gears.

- If you work to apply and invest in improving all your 7 gears, you will earn compound interest.

- As you see now, six of the 7 gears aren't "out there;" they are internal. "As within, so without."

- Summary: When any one (or better yet, ALL) of the 7 gears changes, your whole quality of life experiences and conditions change.

Worth Doing

- Commit to learning at least one useful thing today. Stay enrolled in "MU" (Mobile University) in your car or on your smartphone/mobile device.

- It's time to climb and connect your best opportunity to exciting outcomes and results!

- Work the Collaboration Continuum as often as you can; be mindful that each step requires an investment.

- In order for ANY of what you've learned in *The 7 Gears* to work, you MUST internalize and apply the concepts! Go back and repeat the concepts that are deemed very important!

- Whatever the outcome, result, or effect, take responsibility, because you're still in command of your direction.

- Place enough value on wisdom that you seek it with a passion. King Solomon considered wisdom more profitable and valuable than jewels, silver, or gold. And it's estimated he accumulated 500 tons of solid gold!

- Apply the Pareto 80/20 rule to your best 20 percent.

- Shift your focus off of barriers and gaps and onto outcomes and results.

MAINTENANCE MANUAL

"*The significant problems we face cannot be solved at the same level of thinking we were at when we created them.*"

- Albert Einstein[81]

All 7 Gears Need Attending To

All systems require maintenance, upgrades, or part replacements to stay in good working order. The 7 Gear success *system* is no different in that regard. Rust on any of your gears can slow down your forward-moving progress toward your goals and accomplishments. It can eat up precious time and create frustration and disappointment because one or more of the gears has been neglected or abandoned.

The harmonious alignment of these 7 gears is synergistic in nature; in other words, the combined workings of each gear have an exponential impact on your results and conditions. We discovered the core elements of the **First Cause Gear**, referring to it as the field of Any Possibility and Opportunity, and the Source of

All that is. Matter and energy are in constant interaction and transition. A maximum transfer of opportunity and energy is what this book is about. That is what you will have when you activate and apply *The 7 Gears Between Cause and Effect*.

Barnacles on Your Boat

Doubt, neglect, and negative beliefs or attitudes can accumulate like barnacles on a boat, slowing down your progress. Negative beliefs and attitudes, like barnacles, need to be scraped off the hull of your boat. Keeping vigilant on your thoughts, habits, and beliefs helps minimize junk that may glom onto any of your 7 gears. Keep an eye on your "dashboard" feedback monitoring system. Return often to your Gear 2 Values, Purpose, Goals and Identity at least monthly.

We need to monitor our **Operating Systems** and check our gauges. This applies to our bodies as it does to the internal workings of our 7 gears. We need to keep aware of what our mental/emotional/spiritual **Operating System** is doing to make sure we're still on track. We don't want to drift without correction and system upgrades.

What do my gauges say?

Read Your Gauges

Use your six senses as a "barometer" to report how you feel about each of the gears. **Gear 1, Attention –Awareness,** can serve as an internal meter reader to the full 7-gear system.

A keen sense of Awareness and Attention can monitor the health of your system, alerting you to better opportunities, danger, or an "overheating light" or "check engine" status indicator on your dashboard. If your engine's overheating, you want to know about it. If you have an operating system problem, you want to know about it ASAP.

Keeping Those Gears Turning in the Right Direction

1. If you want to avoid a red alert, simply make it a habit to check on every gear and invest the time to apply all the techniques mentioned here.

2. If you would model the champions, start your lifelong research and study of good books such as those referenced throughout this work. They are your coaches and advisors, waiting to serve you for only a few dollars. Take advantage of the world's best on any subject.

3. As was said in the beginning of this book, you are your best investment. Get sold on the value of investing in you. How many shares of stock do you have in **[Your name], Inc.**? Is [Your name], Inc.'s value going up, as it should?

4. One great personal relationship builder is to promise to your loved one, "I will invest in me for you, if you'll invest in you for me," or, "I'll take care of me for you if you'll take care of you for me." This is a way of proving you care about the relationship. This is not being selfish, because when you work to become the best version of yourself, then you can be more effective in all your activities and eight goal areas.

What's in a Transmission?

In the introduction we used the analogy of an automotive transmission and how its purpose is to convert engine power to the wheels in order to move forward. By now you should have a good grasp of how the 7 Gears <u>transfer and convert internal energy, possibilities, and potential into outward power and movement</u>. The 7 Gears, as you have seen, are part of a "transmission" that transfers torque (force) power and energy from a **Cause**-source to movement and action, delivering an **Effect.** The source of any possibility, Cause, is drawn out with the energy of *focused thoughts* and *emotion*, steered by an **Operating System, Faith-Belief, Perspective**, and **Decision**. From there, the energy is transferred into the physical realm by **Action** delivering **conditions, outcomes, results** or **experiences**—all made to order, your order!

"It's not what happens that determines the major part of your future. What happens, happens to us all. It is what you do about what happens that counts."

- Jim Rohn[82]

The Steering Wheel of Responsibility

When you keep your hands on the steering wheel, you take control. And when you take your hands off the steering wheel, you go to the back of the bus while someone else takes you for a ride, or into the ditch. If you're really serious about tapping into the infinite storehouse of opportunities and converting them to favorable outcomes, results, and experiences, then pay attention to this one! **Putting your hands ON the steering wheel of responsibility shuts down the foolish and useless "blame game"** and squashes the hollow excuses that rob you of opportunity and life's rewards and blessings. Keeping your hands on the

371

responsibility wheel controls and directs your emotions so they don't take you off the road and into the ditch! When you think back to times when you were in control of something like a project or a group, didn't you feel good? Even if it was challenging, it felt good to be in control. This is another side benefit of taking the wheel of responsibility; it just feels good!

As stated in the introduction on prerequisites, the more you repeat material of value and the more you *internalize* the concepts in sequence, the more effective and positive your experiences will be. This is because the purpose of the "change game" is to get through to your subconscious.

Ultimately, our Creator holds the reserved authority to intervene with his plan and fate for our lives. And yet we still carry with us the gifted freedom of choice and responsibility to live with purpose, passion, and direction and to produce, create, and grow, as does all life. Contained within you and me is a responsibility blueprint, a sort of genetic type achievement code. Although we did not come into this world with an operator's manual, we have been purposely gifted six mental faculties as tools and six communication senses to gain the knowledge, skill and ability to operate our equipment, the 7 Gears. All this is for the express intent of carrying out our life's mission and swimming, if you will, across the "pool" described in the preface. We are all participants in a much larger purpose that frames up part of our life mission. Finding the unknown pieces should be viewed as a fun adventure of discovery, like an Easter egg hunt or the popular geocaching search game.

"Life is no brief candle to me. It is a sort of splendid torch which I have got a hold of for the moment, and I want to make it burn as brightly as possible before handing it on to future generations."

- George Bernard Shaw, playwright and Nobel Prize Winner[83]

Call to Action

You have an appointment with an exciting destiny, having now passed through **the 7 Gears between Cause and Effect!** Every decision you make begins change in direction instantly, the results of which may not be noticed until sometime later. Sometimes the change-decision has to be repeated daily in order to take hold as a new habit. Not every change requires days, weeks, months and years to happen. Often the most life-altering changes happen in an instant. Returning one last time to **Gear 6, Decision-Choice, what will you do after you put this book down?**

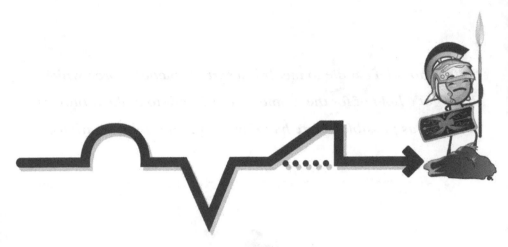

Barriers, Gaps, and Diversions Conquered!

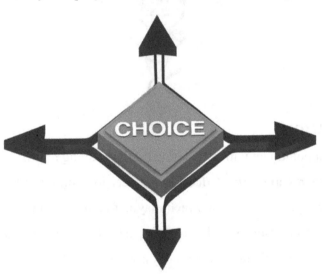

What are you going to do NOW
with YOUR 7 gears?

Take a nap, or take the challenge?

This book does not have all the answers, but it does contain ideas and details that can make THE difference in the quality of your life experiences and standard of living. These 7 gears have the potential to propel you forward in the direction you want to go and connect you to the unlimited opportunities that have been waiting for you! As your coach, I challenge you to grab the brass ring and commit to putting *all* 7 gears into an updated **Daily Action Habit** (DAH) as your **sine qua non!** I trust that you now realize you are capable of much more, now that you've been reacquainted with **your transmission that runs between Cause and Effect.**

Your Diamond Mind

Acres of Diamonds is an enduring classic story written by Russell Conwell in 1915. As the story goes, a young man eager to find diamonds sells his farm to spend the rest of his life searching for them; all the while, the diamonds were in his own back yard. *You* have a diamond mine (or "mind") of opportunities and infinite possibilities waiting to be discovered by your trained eye. You are now like a metal detector; you have the equipment and specialized knowledge of the 7 Gears to better identify, process, and produce the jewels of fabulous outcomes, conditions and life experiences! I trust that you now realize you are capable of tapping into much more opportunity, now that you've been acquainted with your **Cogno-Kinetic system that runs between Cause and Effect**. More important is that you don't just know about these gears, but that you *internalize* them into your Daily Action Habits. Moreover, it's important that you apply these tools into your eight goal areas, defined in Gear 2.

I hope to cross paths with you someday in a seminar or live event so that I can learn about you! I trust you are now are richer and more empowered with the special knowledge of the 7 Gears between Cause and its cumulative effects. Remember, knowledge ***applied*** is power, and it puts you in gear. Huge rewards await you if you apply the gears. I learned a valuable lesson years ago about rereading valuable books. By rereading a good book, you will pick up additional nuggets that you most likely missed from a one-time reading. I challenge you to go back and take another look. You will most likely have another "aha!" moment or see something of value that you missed before. It will be worth it because you will have compounded the return on your investment in this book.

Having passed this way through *The 7 Gears Between Cause and Effect*, may you be blessed with an exciting new level of rewarding experiences, outcomes, and results!

> *"What lies behind you and what lies in front of you,
> pales in comparison to what lies inside of you."*
>
> - Ralph Waldo Emerson

Worth Remembering

- **Like muscle building, repetition of useful information builds mental, emotional, and spiritual strength.**

- **The weakest-running gear may set the pace and level of the other gears before and after it.**

- **All these concepts and more have been waiting for you to discover and apply—that should make you thrilled!**

- There is something *inside you* that wants you to grow, advance and contribute, as does all life. It's time to climb!

- The rewards of investing in your 7 gears will create untold exciting results, outcomes, and life experiences.

- The bum on the street and the billionaire in the board room have the same amount of hours in a day, as do you. How are you investing your irreplaceable minutes? Remember, you can raise the value of your life "chips."

"It used to be about who you know. Now it's what you know, and who knows you."

- T.K. Tolman

Worth Doing

- Avoid the "blame game" like the plague; it's just as deadly. Blaming takes your hands off the steering wheel of responsibility and puts you five steps back on the game board!

- Avoid negative people as if they had a cold virus because negativity is contagious!

- Don't take orders from General-Ality. He'll lead you into the desert and steal your time!

- You are here to fulfill an exciting purpose. Go back to Gear 2 if you're still struggling to find it.

- Commit to Sustained Unwavering Progress through Daily Action Habits—SUPDAH !

- Go back and read the book again and highlight key ideas. Take notes and accelerate the return on your investment to achieve significance and fulfillment in your eight goal areas.

- If life runs on time, then "killing time" is killing life; therefore, seek to *live with love and excitement!* And that's *Sustained Unwavering Progress*, making every moment count, because it does!

- Mastering even one gear will help you immensely; investing in all 7 will give you *exponential* outcomes, results and effects!

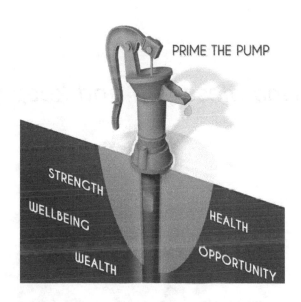

It's time to prime the well pump of unlimited possibility and opportunity that has been waiting for <u>you</u> all along!

May God bless you and keep you!

Recommended Reading:
Books That Cross Paths with One or More of
The 7 Gears

Allen, James. *As a Man Thinketh*. New York: Barnes & Noble, 1992.

Andrews, Andy. *Mastering the Seven Decisions That Determine Personal Success*. Nashville, TN: Thomas Nelson, 2008.

Anthony, Robert. *The Ultimate Secrets of Total Self-Confidence*. New York: Berkley, 1979.

Beckwith, Harry and Christine Clifford Beckwith. *You, Inc.* New York: Warner, 2007.

Canfield, Jack and Janet Switzer. *The Success Principles*. New York: Harper Collins, 2005.

Conwell, Russell. *Acres of Diamonds*. Salt Lake City, UT: Hawkes, 1915.

Duhigg, Charles. *The Power of Habit*. New York: Random, 2014.

Gray, John. *How to Get What You Want and Want What You Have*. New York: Harper Collins, 2000.

Johnson, Spencer. *Who Moved My Cheese?* New York: G.P. Putnam's Sons, 1998.

Kiyosaki, Robert. *Increase Your Financial IQ*. New York: Business Plus, 2008.

Klauser, Henriette Anne. *Write It Down, Make It Happen: Knowing What You Want and Getting It!* New York: Fireside-Simon & Schuster, 2000.

Koch, Richard. *Living the 80/20 Way*. London: Nicholas Brealey, 2004.

Maxwell, John C. *Everyone Communicates; Few Connect*. Nashville, TN: Thomas Nelson, 2010.

Murphy, Joseph. *The Power of Your Subconscious Mind*. Rev. ed. Paramus,NJ: Reward, 2000.

Niven, David. *The 100 Simple Secrets of Successful People*. New York: Harper, 2002.

Proctor, Bob. *It's Not About the Money*. Toronto: Burman, 2009.

Robbins, Anthony. *Awaken the Giant Within*. New York: Summit, 1991.

Rohn, Jim. *Seven Strategies for Wealth and Happiness*. Rocklin, CA: Prima, 1986.

Tracey, Brian. *Goals!* San Francisco, CA: Barrett-Koehler, 2010.

NOTES

[1] Bristol, Claude M. *The Magic of Believing*. 1948. New York: Cornerstone-Simon & Schuster, 1973. 189.

[2] Covey, Stephen R. *The 7 Habits of Highly Effective People*. New York: Fireside-Simon & Schuster, 1990. and Frankl, Viktor. *Man's Search for Meaning*. Boston: Beacon, 1959.

[3] Allen, James. *As a Man Thinketh*. New York: Barnes & Noble, 1992. 3.

[4] Ziglar, Zig. *See You at the Top*. Gretna, LA: Pelican, 1983, 6.

[5] Allen, 3.

[6] Allen, 3.

[7] Allenbaugh, Eric. *Wake-Up Calls – You Don't Have to Sleepwalk Through Your Life, Love or Career!* New York: Fireside-Simon & Schuster, 1994. 74.

[8] Hersey, William D. *How to Cash In on Your Hidden Memory Power*. New York: Prentice Hall, 1963. 21.

[9] Attributed to Aristotle on "Aristotle." BrainyQuote.com. Xplore Inc., 2015. 13 April 2015. http://www.brainyquote.com/quotes/quotes/a/aristotle132267.html

[10] Behrend, Genevieve. *Your Invisible Power*. Radford, VA: Wilder, 2007. 7.

[11] *The Holy Bible: New International Version*. Grand Rapids, MI: Zondervan, 1984.

[12] Murphy, Joseph. *The Power of Your Subconscious Mind*. Paramus, NJ: Reward, 2000. 42.

[13] *The Wizard of Oz*. Dir. Victor Fleming. Perf. Judy Garland, Frank Morgan, Ray Bolger, Bert Lahr, Jack Haley, Billy Burke, Margaret Hamilton, Charley Grapewln. Metro-Goldwyn-Mayer, 1939. DVD.

[14] "James Thurber Quotes." NotableQuotes.com. 15 April 2015. http://www.notable-quotes.com/t/thurber_james.html, from Thurber, James. *Credos and Curios*. 1962.

[15] Goddard, Neville. *The Power of Awareness*. Altenmunster, Germany: Jazzybee. 2012. 16, 23.

[16] Allen 13.

[17] Yate, Martin. *Beat the Odds: Career Buoyancy Tactics for Today's Turbulent Job Market*. New York: Ballantine, 1995. 18.

[18] Rodgers McCoy, V., Adult Development. Retrieved November 13, 2014, http://www.uwyo.edu/aded5050/5050unit4/intro.asp

[19] Hill, Napoleon and Annie Lou Norman Hill. *How to Raise Your Own Salary*. Chicago, IL: Napoleon Hill Assoc., 1953. 17, 21.

[20] Quote from American McGee's *Alice*, video game, 2000. Developed by Rogue Entertainment. Published, distributed and marketed by Electronic Arts.

[21] Wattles, Wallace. *The Science of Getting Rich*. Lakemont, GA: CSA, 1975.

[22] *The Science of Getting Rich*. Dir. Michael Jeffreys, DVD. Seminar Apps DTN Int'l. 2011

[23] *"Robert Byrne Quotes." Quotes.net.* STANDS4 LLC, 2015. Web. 15 Apr. 2015. http://www.quotes.net/quote/5216.

[24] Brodie, Richard. *Getting Past OK: A Straightforward Guide to Having a Fantastic Life.* Seattle: Integral, 1993. 51.

[25] Boyd, Ty. "Excellence in Speaking Institute Promotion." High Country Business Network. *YouTube,* July 7, 2008. Web. 18 November 2014.

[26] Gates, Bill. "Long-Term View Helps Businesses Focus on Success." *Daily News,* Los Angeles, CA. 23 July 1995: n. pag. *HighBeam Research.* Web. 23 April 2015. http://www.highbeam.com/doc/1P2-25012146.html

[27] Tracy, Brian. *Goals!* San Francisco, CA: Berrett-Koehler, 2010. 2.

[28] *The Science of Getting Rich.* Dir. Michael Jeffreys, DVD. Seminar Apps DTN Int'l. 2011

[29] Kopmeyer, M.R. *How You Can Get Richer Quicker.* Kingsport, TN: M.R. Kopmeyer, 1975. 159.

[30] Hill, Napoleon. *Think and Grow Rich.* Greenwich, CT: Fawcett, 1960. 52.

[31] Senay, Ibrahim, Dolores Albarracin, and Kenji Nogichi. "Motivating Goal-Directed Behavior Through Introspective Self-Talk: The Role of the Interrogative Form of Simple Future Tense." *Psychological Science.* 2010 Apr. 21(4):499-504. doi: 10.1177/0956797610364751. Epub 2010 Mar 9.

[32] *The Holy Bible, King James Version.* Cambridge Edition: 1769; *King James Bible Online,* 2015. http://www.kingjamesbibleonline.org/

[33] *The Holy Bible: New International Version.* Grand Rapids, MI: Zondervan, 1984.

[34] William James (1842-1910) was an American psychologist and leader of the philosophical movement of Pragmatism.

[35] Ailes, Roger. *You Are the Message: Getting What You Want by Being Who You Are.* New York: Doubleday, 1988. 112.

[36] *The Holy Bible, King James Version.* Cambridge Edition: 1769; *King James Bible Online,* 2015. http://www.kingjamesbibleonline.org/

[37] Attributed to Reinhold Niebuhr (1892-1971)

[38] Quoted in Collier, Robert. *The Secret of Power.* New York: Start, 2012. 36.

[39] Coelho, Paul. "You can become blind by seeing each day as a similar one. Each day is a different one; each day brings a miracle of its own. It's just a matter of paying attention to this miracle." Facebook. January 24, 2010. [15 April 2015 < https://www.facebook.com/paulocoelho/posts/307410088081>].

[40] "Science Quotes by Charles F. Kettering." Todayinsci.com. Today in Science History, 1999-2015. 22 April 2015. http://www.todayinsci.com/K/Kettering_Charles/KetteringCharles-Quotations.htm

[41] Robbins, Anthony. *Awaken the Giant Within.* New York: Summit, 1991. 188.

[42] Quoted in Hill, Napoleon and Annie Lou Norman Hill. *How to Raise Your Own Salary. Chicago, IL:* Napoleon Hill Assoc., 1953. 78.

[43] Ziglar, 203.

[44] Wattles, Wallace. *The Science of Getting Rich.* Lakemont, GA: CSA, 1975. 77.

[45] "Lead the Field." Chicago: Conant Publishing, 1990. Print. Audio Transcript. p. 8.

[46] Byrne, Rhonda. *The Secret*. Hillsboro, OR: Beyond Words-Simon & Schuster, 2006. 37.

[47] Ponder, Catherine. *Open Your Mind to Receive*. Marina del Ray, CA: Devross, 1983. 92.

[48] Hopkins, Tom. *The Official Guide to Success*. 1982. Reprint. New York: Warner, 1984. 23.

[49] "Eleanor Roosevelt." Goodreads.com. Goodreads, Inc., 2015. 22 April 2015. http://www.goodreads.com/author/quotes/44566.Eleanor_Roosevelt, taken from Roosevelt, Eleanor. *You Learn by Living: Eleven Keys for a More Fulfilling Life*. New York: Harper, 1960.

[50] Proctor, Bob and Michele Blood. *Become a Magnet to Money*. La Jolla, CA: Musivation Int'l., 2008. 73.

[51] Fredrickson, Barbara. *Positivity*. New York: Random, 2009. 84.

[52] Rohn, Jim. *Seven Strategies for Wealth and Happiness*. Rocklin, CA: Prima, 1986. 12.

[53] Quoted in Kopmeyer, 28.

[54] "Julie Andrews." BrainyQuote.com. Xplore Inc., 2015. 31 March 2015. http://www.brainyquote.com/quotes/authors/j/julie_andrews.html

[55] Tracy 176.

[56] Anderson, U.S. *The Magic in Your Mind*. New York: Thomas Nelson & Sons, 1961. 1.

[57] Murphy, Shane. *The Achievement Zone*. New York: Berkley, 1996. 4.

[58] O'Connor, Joseph and Ian McDermott. *Principles of NLP*. San Francisco, CA: Harper-Collins Thorsons, 1996. 50-51.

[59] Davis, Gayle A. *High Performance Thinking*. Colorado Springs, CO: Quality, 1999, p ix.

[60] Davis, 2.

[61] Maltz, Maxwell. *Psycho-Cybernetics*. Hollywood, CA: Wilshire, 1969.

[62] Matthew 5:45.*The Holy Bible: New International Version*. Grand Rapids, MI: Zondervan, 1984.

[63] Chandler, Steve. *100 Ways to Motivate Yourself: Change Your Life Forever*. Franklin Lakes, NJ: Career, 2004. 62.

[64] Tracy, Brian. *Maximum Achievement*. New York: Simon & Schuster, 1993. 86, 87.

[65] Distinguished professor of psychology at Claremont University Mihaly Csikszentmihályi and other scientists and researchers, including Steven Kotler and Jamie Wheal, co-founders of the Flow Genome Project, have taken a modern scientific look at how to obtain joyfully motivating moments of high performance. Interestingly, being in the "flow" or "zone" has been known by other names in many cultures throughout history.

[66] Wenger, Win, and Richard Poe. *The Einstein Factor: A Proven New Method for Increasing Your Intelligence*. Rocklin, CA: Prima, 1996. 250.

[67] Hill 64.

[68] Rowling, J.K. "The Fringe Benefits of Failure, and the Importance of Imagination." 2008, June 5. Speech presented at Harvard University, Cambridge, MA.

[69] Zuckerberg, Mark. Interview. Startup School 2011, Stanford University. October 30, 2011.

[70] Bristol, Claude M. and Harold Sherman. *TNT: The Power Within You*. Englewood Cliffs, NJ: Prentice Hall, 1954. 117.

[71] McKenna, Paul. *I Can Make You Confident: The Power to Go for Anything You Want!* New York: Sterling, 2010. 124.

[72] Tice, Louis E. *Smart Talk for Achieving Your Potential: 5 Steps to Get You from Here to There*. Seattle, WA: Pacific Inst., 1995. 173.

[73] *The Holy Bible: New International Version*. Grand Rapids, MI: Zondervan, 1984.

[74] Gittelson, Bernard. *How to Make Your Own Luck*. New York: Warner, 1981. 30.

[75] Allen 3.

[76] Jobs, Steve. "How to Live Before You Die." 2005, June 12. Speech presented at Stanford University, Stanford, CA.

[77] Allen 20.

[78] Koch, Richard. *Living the 80/20 Way: Work Less, Worry Less, Succeed More, Enjoy More*. Yarmouth, ME: Nicholas Brealey, 2004.

[79] Fehrenbacher, Don E., and Virginia Fehrenbacher, eds. *Recollected Words of Abraham Lincoln*. Stanford, CA: Stanford UP, 1996. 33.

[80] Adams, Brian. *How to Succeed: Dynamic Mind Principles That Transform Your Life*. Hollywood, CA: Melvin Powers Wilshire, 1985. 24.

[81] Quoted in Covey, Stephen R. *The 7 Habits of Highly Effective People*. New York: Fireside-Simon & Schuster, 1990. 42.

[82] Rohn, Jim. *The Treasury of Quotes*. Lake Dallas, TX: Success, 1994-2010. 116.

[83] "George Bernard Shaw." izQuotes.com. Iz Quotes, 2015. 15 April 2015. http://izquotes.com/quote/333371, taken from *Bernard Shaw: Selections of His Wit and Wisdom*. Harnsberger, Caroline Thomas, Ed. Follett, 1965. 179.

Thomas Tolman is a writer, speaker, and creator of *The 7 Gears Program* that focuses on leadership, high-performance business collaboration, and personal growth.

Born and raised in Colorado, Tom began a career in radio and television broadcasting, then moved into public safety communications as director of national projects. He has led multiple award-winning programs through the University of Denver Research Institute and other national initiatives.

Tom has authored numerous research-based works and has served as a guest presenter for IT industry associations, the FCC, the U.S. State House and Senate, The National Press Club, and various universities. He holds a B.S. in Business Management and a Master's degree in Technology Management from the University of Denver.

For an audio version of this book, more information, or to book Tom as a speaker, visit www.the7gears.com.